The Cabot Trail

in Black and White

"**Listen.** You can tell people about this. But don't tell them everything. If people knew what we have here, we wouldn't be able to afford the ground we're standing on."

—in conversation with
the Smith brothers
on the North River

Tommy and Josie MacDonald,
French River

INTRODUCTION

A ROAD IS BOTH LIMITATIONS AND POSSIBILI-TIES. For me, for over 25 years, travelling with a tape recorder and camera, the Cabot Trail was a major route toward the making of *Cape Breton's Magazine.* My Cabot Trail, of course, included a mix of backlands, highlands and intervales—really the main highway and its environs—a community linked throughout northern Cape Breton, from Middle River to Bay St. Lawrence, Wreck Cove to Chéticamp, Englishtown, the Margarees and White Point.

Smokey and French and MacKenzie Mountains were barriers and accomplishments. The Highlands plateau and the ride from Ingonish to Aspy Bay, inland or coastal, simply incredible luxuries. And no matter how difficult I thought it might be—how cold or steep or windy or lonely—it never seemed much compared to those who managed it on foot, in the darkness and snow and fog, delivering mail or fighting crime or answering a call for help—or just fighting for a living, day after day, building community and home.

These selections tell part of the story. The photographs give us an additional way in. Still, we ask how they did it, how they managed.

I once asked my hero Roddy Hector Mac-Donald—a man I watched day after day winning the hay, chopping huge piles of winter wood, mending fences, saying his prayers, enjoying hot fires in the kitchen and a strong cup of tea. We were standing at the barn door, looking out at the beating rain, the horse and cow and chickens fed behind us.

I thought this was the moment. "Roddie," I asked him. "How did they do it, the old people?" And this competent, humble man never turned to me, never moved. Looking straight into the rain he said, "Well, isn't that just it?"

Ronald Caplan
Wreck Cove

The Cabot Trail · - · - ·

THE
Cabot Trail
IN BLACK & WHITE

**Voices and 150 Photographs
from Northern Cape Breton**

Ronald Caplan

Breton Books

Editor: Ronald Caplan
Production Assistance: Bonnie Thompson
James Fader, Fader Communications

Our Thanks: *Cape Breton's Magazine* was only possible with the generous help of hundreds of people. For this book, specifically, we want to thank the following: Photographer Carol Kennedy who, along with James Fader, helped us create the front cover photo of Donald (Little Donald) and Dan Murdoch Morrison holding a photo of their sister Maisie, Wreck Cove. Back cover photographs, clockwise from top left: Minnie Aucoin, St. Joseph du Moine; Wishie Rose, Baddeck; hauling a mackerel net off Ingonish; Hattie Carmichael, St. Ann's; Dennis and Alexander Smith coming ashore, and John William Morrison in the winch house, Wreck Cove; and John A. Wilkie, Sugarloaf, and Effie Fitzgerald, Aspy Bay. Clarence Barrett's stories about the fox and the whales are from his book, *Cape Breton Highlands National Park: A Park Lover's Companion*. Bill Fraser's walk around the Cabot Trail is taken from R. A. MacLean's taped conversations made in the preparation of his book, *Bill Fraser: Mountie*. Stories from the Clyburn Valley were collected by Maureen Scobie and *Cape Breton's Magazine*.

Pam Doyle, Glenn King, Delores Neal and James Bridgeland from the Cape Breton Highlands National Park provided park information regarding the Clyburn Valley. Historian Ken Donovan supplied the golf photographs on pages 32 and 35 [courtesy Highlands Links], as well as pictures of the Donovan and Doucette homes in the Clyburn Valley [courtesy Parks Canada].

Ken also shared Wilfred Creighton's photos of houses expropriated in creating the Cape Breton Highlands National Park. The men fishing lobsters with Johnny MacInnes were Merrill MacInnis, Sandy Greig, and Peter Darnell. The photo of Chéticamp Harbour in 1925, and the quote on page 16, are from Fr. Anselme Chiasson's book *Chéticamp: History and Acadian Traditions*.

Steve Whitty's rendition of "Going to the Harvest" appeared in *Cape Breton's Magazine* and in A. A. (Tony) MacKenzie's book, *The Harvest Train*. Photo on page 57 is courtesy of Provincial Archives of Manitoba; page 58 courtesy of Mabou Gaelic and Historical Society. Owen Fitzgerald was the principal photographer the night of the milling frolic in Josie and Tommy MacDonald's house, French River. Frank Speck's interviews were first published in the *Journal of American Folklore* in 1915. Dr. Ken Murray gave us a printed version of Dr. Léo LeBlanc's trek from the *Nova Scotia Medical Journal*, 1936; and Clara Mae and Georgette Samson, daughter and granddaughter of Dr. LeBlanc, supplied the photograph. Theresa MacDonald (wife of John D. MacDonald), her daughter Lisa, and Theresa's sister Rose Burton saved and shared Duncan H. MacDonald's extraordinary letter. Pam Newton, Point Edward, first suggested we talk with Lexie O'Hare, and Anne Comfort Morrell, Big Intervale, helped make that visit possible.

We acknowledge the support of the Canada Council for the Arts for our publishing program.

Canada Council for the Arts   Conseil des Arts du Canada

We acknowledge support from Cultural Affairs, Nova Scotia Department of Tourism, Culture and Heritage.

NOVA SCOTIA
Tourism, Culture and Heritage

We acknowledge the financial support of the Government of Canada through the Book Publishing Industry Development Program (BPIDP) for our publishing activities.

Canadä

Library and Archives Canada Cataloguing in Publication

Caplan, Ronald, 1942-
        The Cabot Trail in black and white : voices and photographs from northern Cape Breton / Ronald Caplan.

ISBN 978-1-895415-99-5

        1. Cabot Trail (N.S.)—History. 2. Cabot Trail (N.S.)—Pictorial works. 3. Cape Breton Island (N.S.)—Biography. 4. Oral history—Nova Scotia—Cape Breton Island. I. Title.

FC2343.4.C36 2007   971.6'91   C2007-902885-3

Printed in Canada

CONTENTS CONTINUE ON NEXT PAGE

Roddy Hector MacDonald,
Wreck Cove

Jack Ingraham— Fish and "Good Rock"

RIGHT HERE IN NEIL'S HARBOUR was a great place for fishing. In the spring and the fall—the fish would be going down in the spring, you know, going up in the Gulf of St. Lawrence; and in the fall when it start getting cold, they come back. And you get two good cracks at them. Well, boats from everywhere—even boats from the States—would be down here fishing off in the fall. But they had to fish outside three mile. But from Lunenburg and Newfoundland—schooners—I don't know how many boats....

There was a pile of fish took in, I'll tell you. Right here in this little place. Mostly all small boats. I think there'd be days I think a hundred thousand would come in here—pounds. I know they had a boat—a collecting boat used to take them to North Sydney—and she took 80,000 pounds, and there's lots of days she couldn't take them all. Wonderful catches of fish.

I think probably about 100 years since Newfoundlanders came here to Neil's Harbour. They came for fishing. You know, the fish was thousands here then. And there was a fella came there from St. Ann's—Buchanan and MacLeod—set up a fish business. Buy fish, and grocery store—oh, they had a big business. Anywhere's a Newfoundlander can go to sell fish, he didn't care where it was at.

Good rock. If there was good rock, to build his house on—he didn't care about land at all.

And all the good places there was, with good land—they picked this way. They weren't looking at land—it was somebody to buy fish.

It was all rocks where they come from. There were cows, keep chickens—some people would have a little garden but they give it up—the land is hard to work. Take the sod off, nothing but rock underneath.

It'll grow hay. There's nowheres in the world

grass'll grow like it. You go down on some of the farms and here's the grass about six inches high. Grow that in nearly two weeks. The vapour off of the salt water probably does it. Cattle was always in, you know, pretty shape—you talk about a great place for cattle.

Trade codfish for potatoes. People didn't mind working for a little bit of money, you know? Now, people's crazy. Well, there's people making 30, 34, 35 dollars a day—going around striking for more money—but by god that was a month's wages. You're darn right. Yes, sir. A month's wages [one time], that 36 dollars. They're striking, and if they get some more, prices all go up and they got to pay rent and income tax—and they don't end up with a bit more than when

they were making 30 dollars a month. Had no money then and they got none now.

I FISHED FROM WHEN I WAS 14 YEARS OLD, and I quit when I was 60. I had to quit. I fished in a rowboat first, no motor at all—the first three to four years. I was fishing haddock. You'd catch more fish in a rowboat then than you can catch now in a big one. Used to get two and three thousand pound in a day. After they were split, you know. We only had four lines of trawl. Just, I suppose, it'd be 300 yards off the shore. Close in to the shore, haddock would school right along the shore. And four lines, floated, with floats on them, about eight fathom under water.

When they were biting, you'd just pull it in and take them off and run it out again. Two runs and the boats we had carried about 1200 pounds. That's two good runs would load them. There was an awful lot caught. Then they got traps. Fish traps.

First, there was no sale for fresh fish—it was all salt. Salt them and dry them. And they never stopped from the time they put the trap out. Every day they worked till sundown. Same the next, day after day. Salting fish and drying them. Then it would be September before they'd get them dry. There was no such a thing as wondering if they'd get any haddock. Their trap would be full all the time.

After a while they got cold storage and they started buying fresh fish. Take them to the cold storage and make fillets. That'd be Sydney and Halifax. The boats would come to Ingonish and pick up the fish. Different days one trap company would get 100,000 pounds of haddock. Half cent a pound. Now that got scarcer and scarcer since the draggers are cleaning them up everywhere. They're pretty near a thing of the past now.

Now they catch nothing but mackerel. I don't know if they ever did get a haddock or not this year in Ingonish. No more haddock. Now, if they get them they get about 12 cents a pound for them. It always seems like anything's a good price, you can't get it. That's the way it is with fishing, huh?

Uncle Reuben

UNCLE REUBEN—he made a sealing trip one time out to the ice, around the first of March. You know, you've seen the drift ice, I suppose. They left here in this little boat, she was only 12 ton—no engine or anything—and they got off so far, and they got stuck in the ice.

And they got out of that and they kept on going to Newfoundland. They got a few seals. They sold them in Newfoundland to get some grub and stuff aboard the boat. Then they got into ice over there, you know, and it come to blow. Come a norther. Oh, blow a gale. There was another big schooner beside them in the ice. And they drove away. And when the blow was over, they had left Newfoundland and they were 50 miles off Scatarie. Things were pretty bad for them in the ice, and the boat leaking—so they left their boat and they went aboard the Newfoundland schooner. Took what seals they had. They gave it to the Newfoundlander. He took them back to Newfoundland. And they got back home here sometime in June.

And every year—I always used to go down to Uncle Reuben's place. He had a house there where the doctor's office is. I'd go down there pretty often. And every year, for 10 or 15 years in a row, on the first of March, he'd tell me all about that trip. I got his picture in the house, too. Uncle Reuben....

The Great Pleasant Bay Fire—1947

MARY FRASER, *Pleasant Bay*: I was the telephone operator. That was my job. I remember that morning that the superintendent from Ingonish came, and he had the longest telegram. The telegraph office was down the road about a mile from here. So he brought me this up. I sent that off for him, telling about the fire. He asked me, "Mrs. Fraser," he said, "would you be willing to stay as long as you can?" "Yes," I said, "I'll stay as long as anybody else stays around here." So he went off. There was an old priest in Chéticamp at the time, Fr. LeBlanc, he was calling me every half hour—"How is the fire now, Mrs. Fraser? Oh well be careful now," he'd say, "and don't stay too long." I said, "No, I'll be safe enough." Then it was the R.C.M.P. that came that day. And he asked me if I'd stay, and I said, "Yes." So then we had our lunch, and I had washed the dishes, and the R.C.M.P. came running up the hill again. He said, "You'd better get ready now, because it's getting too close"—that was around one o'clock in the afternoon. So we got ready. We had two cabins down in the field there, so we took a lot of stuff down here—we were sure our house would burn, anyway. And we left.

That was the last day, anyway. It was on a Monday. See, on the Friday before, the fire flew up out of the river and we could see it right up there, going by—there was this pink light that the fire cast—and we thought we were safe. But of course, it was still smouldering. Saturday, everything was fine. I mean, it was a nice quiet day, and we thought we were all right. Of course, we went to church on Sunday down here. Sunday evening, I saw a lot of the cars from after church come up to the mountain there to see the fire—it seemed to be burning pretty bad then—they were up to watch this fire. In the morning everybody knew that it couldn't miss

Mary and Rod Fraser

us. There were people in all kinds of trucks and cars. They were calling people to come to fight the fire, and there was a bunch out here that Monday morning, way up on top of the mountain there, fighting the fire. And they pretty near got caught up there—young men—some of them weren't, but most of them were from up here. They were carrying the water up there on their backs—such a job.

And I remember when we were going up the mountain here, leaving in the car, just after we passed the bridge here, the park superintendent met us. We said, "Looks pretty bad." He said, "Yes." He said, "We're going to try and save your house—you have such a lovely home down here." But before he got back down, the house was gone. But we had gone to Chéticamp then; we stopped at Mary Bourgeois' there. She had been calling us and calling us to come and stay with them—they knew we were going to have to leave here. So we went up there. Mr. Bourgeois, he had been down here that afternoon. When he got home, he wouldn't come in the house at all, because he hated to come in and tell us that our house was gone.

ROD FRASER: The fire started here in August 1947. **MARY**: It had been simmering out on the mountain there for a couple weeks, Rod, hadn't it? **ROD**: Yes, it was burning on MacKenzie Mountain way out for a week and a half before it came down here. I don't think it's ever been known how it started. It was no hunting season at all. It started out MacKenzie River a good two miles from where you cross the bridge, in a place it was almost impossible to get to. And if it had been down at the riverbed, you would say it was some tourist was out there fishing or something, that started it. But it started way up on the side of the mountain. Well, a mountain goat might get up there.

I know the spot. There were a lot of old pine trees out there that had fallen down, old dry stumps. And I know we had a lightning storm just a few days before that. I was the first one that saw the fire. I was coming over from Chéticamp—but of course, they didn't pay much attention to it first. You saw the smoke, but there were no trails then, no way to get at it. They *couldn't* fight it. They were just praying for rain. Instead of that, it was gradually getting worse.

Of course, when it came down close, they started fighting it with water. They had pumps, the Park Department, they were over here from Ingonish—they had all their fighting equipment and everything over here. But you couldn't do anything with that fire.

I'll tell you now how fast it travelled. You've been by the church down there, haven't you? We lived up here on the hill, just above here. And our house went afire—I wasn't here at the time—

Rod Fraser

I'd taken the wife and daughter up to Chéticamp—everybody was ordered out of here. But the superintendent of the park told me our house, when it caught, and before the roof fell in, the church was afire down there. **MARY**: You know, there was an awful gale of wind, and the fire was just going through the air. It had wind and hot sun. **ROD**: It was just one of those days when there was a gale of west wind. The ocean was right white. And there hadn't been a drop of rain for over two months. Everything was just dry and scorching. It had everything that a fire needed, everything that it needed to burn.

MARY: And you know, it didn't matter where it dropped, it burned—except down there at the cemetery. There was a fire started there—a tree in there that burnt—and then went out. Wasn't that fortunate? It didn't burn the cemetery. But everywhere else burnt. **ROD**: The grass in the cemetery didn't burn at all. Change of wind, I guess. **MARY**: Oh, God knows what it was. And there were some woods, where the woods are down there now, they didn't burn, none of that on that little point down there—burned around it.

ROD: So we left here when everybody was ordered out, you know. I imagine there were 35 or 40 families left. Mostly everybody that could go, went. Of course, there were a few of the men stayed here, but all the womenfolks went out. I think we were the second last car that left here. And it was so hot going up MacKenzie Mountain that I had to keep the windows up to keep the heat out of the car.

MARY: Well, I'll tell you, that the fire then was just coming out of the river when we drove through, and it was coming so fast up the river, it just looked like the train was coming up there. So fast.

ROD: When I started to take the wife and daughter through, I started with the idea of getting back here again. But I couldn't get back. I dropped them off in Chéticamp and I turned right around and made for home. But I met people said you couldn't get through, the fire was all over the road, everything was burnt. It wasn't a paved road then. But this was on the Cabot Trail. So I went back to Chéticamp then and we hired a motorboat, myself and the mailman down here, John MacGregor, hired one of those big longliners—there happened to be a couple of them in the harbour. And the fellow who took us down on the boat, he died about a week ago—Peter Larade. And when we got down here, you couldn't see Pleasant Bay for smoke.

First thing I saw was the driftwood down on the beach, burning—I knew then that everything was gone. And the smoke was so thick, we couldn't tell where we were, we couldn't get near the wharf—there was no harbour here then. And it was rough, blowing just a terrible gale. We found out after a while where we were, and we got one boatload—somebody came out in a rowboat and took out a couple that were sick—they were miserable, you know. And one of them died in the hospital a couple days later. One boatload, and then we had to pull out of there.

There were women and children down there, waiting to get out, people that didn't get away by land. Picked up what we could, but we had to leave there, we couldn't take them all; we couldn't get ashore. So there were a lot of people spent the night on the beach, all night. We took what we could back to Chéticamp.

We didn't get back here for a week afterwards. It was burning around here all the time. Everything was black. The fields were black—the heather fields were all burnt and scorched—everything was as black as the top of the stove. Everything was burnt. Just one building up here that stood. I think in all there were about 17 houses burnt here in about an hour and a half. There was nothing left this side of Timmons' store, only just

two family houses. Bishop family saved their house, and the Moores over here. Fire went all around it, but he kept water pouring on it all the time, and when he had to get out, he left the hose running on the roof—and I guess that saved the house. And in Red River, it went down as far as just beyond the church. The school

Willard Hinkley

didn't burn. The *old* schoolhouse—*that* burnt—the old hall. There was a store there—that burnt. And there were three homes that burnt there, and just everything you touched was smoke.

MARY: We lost two pigs, that was all our animals that were lost. The other animals stood in the brook down there by our barn. They wandered along the brook, and they didn't get burnt. The horse stood up in the brook there. And our neighbour the next morning went up looking for her. And he had an awful job to coax this mare to come out, because she was so frightened, the poor thing, she just shook and shivered. But she wasn't a bit hurt, for all that, which was a wonderful thing. But our neighbour down here, two of his cows got burnt.

ROD: But he didn't lose them. Their feet got scorched, but they were all right. There was nobody got hurt. It happened in the daytime, that was just the only thing. There were old people here. If the fire would have struck here in the night, it would have been pretty hard to get them out.

WILLARD HINKLEY, *Pleasant Bay*: It came across the mountain when it did break out, came out above the Bonnie Doon Motel up there. We fought it out there. We were out there for four or five days, with the park warden and voluntary firemen from around here. We had a volun-

tary fire ranger for the Provincial, and he went around and asked you to go and fight fire. So we all did. But nobody ever dreamt that it would ever come into the community. See, we got it under control up there at Beach Hill, we call it. We figured it was pretty good. Using back tanks and firehose and pumping engines from the brook. (*It wasn't a big fire then?*) No, it was more or less burning in the sods, in the turf and things like that. Then the wind hauled southwest. And she came out MacKenzie River—she came out that river just like a gunshot. The fire was about half a mile ahead of the smoke—the blaze, where it was just sifting through. We found it impossible to do anything there.

We were there I think 11 days altogether, fighting it—and you'd think it was under control, and the first thing you'd know, bang-o, away it'd come again.

I was in Red River when it came around the second time. It went through the first time, and then it was about two days we were just there watching any fires that would flare up. We'd sleep on the floor in some of the houses. And some nights you'd be up all night—you'd sleep a little in the daytime when somebody else'd be watching the fire. Keep spraying the

Jack Sam Hinkley

burnt ground and the burnt trees—any little wind that would come up would start this all up again. And after the trees were burnt, the leaves and all the needles burnt off of them—well, they were just skeletons. Now if that started up again, that'd burn twice as bad, because that stuff would be just as dry as powder.

Then about on the third day, another strip came through—a strip two or three hundred feet wide from the burnt part down—and the rabbits and the deer and everything were running ahead of that—just whistling. You could see those rabbits going by, just sizzling. And the deer they were right tame. They'd run right up to you. It seemed as if they wanted your protection.

JOHN SAM (JACK SAM) HINKLEY, *Pleasant Bay*: We had a house and a barn over there, and they both got burnt. And I had ten cords of sawed-up wood ready for the stove. I had it put in the woodhouse. I had just put it in the day before, finished it. Put it in for the winter. It was dry, you know. And there was about as much outside there, too. And it burned that, too. The whole house and everything. I never saved anything. I had a couple of rifles. I took them down and put them in the potato field—buried them up in the ground there. I saved them. And that's about all I saved. And a few trunks of clothes. Hauled them out in a field— I saved them. The fire ran all over the fields, same as anywhere else. Same as it did in the woodland. Dry weather for a long time. Terrible dry weather.

The Red Cross came into Chéticamp and they set up in buildings and tents there, put the

The Great Pleasant Bay Fire—1947

Walter Moore

people all in tents for a few days. The most of the people went to Chéticamp. Couldn't go to Cape North—they were not much better than here. Just Chéticamp was the handiest place. And we did all our business in Chéticamp. They used us wonderful. The French people used us awful good.

(*Did anything good come out of that fire?*) No. I don't think. It even stunted the potatoes, the potatoes weren't much that fall. Burnt the tops off or they'd have grown more.

WALTER MOORE, *Red River*: We had the pumps hooked up to a couple of brooks, ready to fight that fire—but when the fire hit in, we couldn't do a thing. There was a roar, you would think there were half a dozen trains coming through. It struck two or three houses there, and we couldn't even get near those houses. We went over the bank to the ocean to get our breath. I knew there was nothing we could do, and I walked down the beach clean down to where the church is. When I was coming down the beach, I saw all kinds of animals on the beach, rabbits, I saw a partridge with all the feathers burned off him. It was just wicked. Came up the bank there. We had some more pumps down there. But I came to the conclusion there was just nothing at all we could do, so I started home to try to take stuff out of the house. I even threw stuff out the window—never even bothered to put the window up—because I was so sure the house was going to burn. Then we had to leave there, too, and go down to the ocean again.

WILLARD HINKLEY: That mountain up there was handsome, all big maple and birch, trees 75 feet high, I suppose, without a limb, some of them. Just like walking under a big roof in there. It looks nice now because everything is grown back and is green, but you could go for a walk then through the woods. Now you can't get anywhere unless you're on the trail, a mass of thick little trees. It looks nice, but it doesn't look a bit like before it burned.

Shotgun fence, Margaree

Shovelling the Snow off Smokey Mountain

DANNY MACASKILL, *Breton Cove*: I started to deliver the mail in July 1923. From Englishtown to Ingonish Ferry. I'd go over Smokey Mountain. I used to cross the ferry at Englishtown. It was awkward. When I started it was only a one-car ferry. Once the fall of the year would come, a windy day or anything like that, the ferry wouldn't work, couldn't get across—you'd have to wait up there at Jersey Cove till you'd get the ferry. Well around Christmas they were hauling the ferryboat up and they were ferrying with a rowboat. And when the drift ice would come, that was gone—couldn't ferry anymore with the rowboat itself. So you had to depend on the ice, harbour ice. Cross from Jersey Cove to Englishtown with a horse and sleigh. And sometimes you'd have to go on very poor ice, too. In the spring of the year, drift ice would be in and there'd be no ferry and you'd have to try to get the mail across some way, any way—and you'd risk going on very poor ice. I never had any trouble with it—but I was on very poor ice, poor going.

Then in the winter, a stormy day, when it was snowing and blowing from the east, you'd have to watch very carefully or else you'd get lost on the ice. You couldn't see where you were going. Sometimes the ice wouldn't be bushed early. Then when they had the bushes on, when you were going up Jersey Cove you had to watch you didn't go too far out or else you'd never find the bushes. There was nobody lost there as far as I know, but there was a couple of horses drowned there. Got lost like that and they went in the entrance [of the harbour]. The tide keeps the ice broke up above the government wharf. And sometimes there'd be slush ice going and it'd fill in against the other ice, and I guess that's what fooled them. They went on that slush ice and the horses got in the ice.

I saw one winter here, Smokey Mountain blocked up with snow and there was no mail going across—just the year before I started driving the mail—it was Dan Urquhart then. Christmas Day the mountain was blocked. And there was no more mail went down till sometime in April, by boat. They couldn't do a thing. There was no traffic through there at all. The only way you'd get through there was on snowshoes. And when we started with the mail, it was bad—but we used to keep it open. We used to have fellows down there in Wreck Cove working for us, breaking the road there.

(*Did they plow?*) Oh, no—shovelling it.

8

Shovel the snow away. Boy, they'd have cuts in it about four feet deep. (*How long?*) It was from the foot of Smokey to the top. It had almost to be shovelled every bit of it to get a horse to go through it. And even so you were leaving a lot of snow. And maybe a couple of days time the darn thing would plug up again on you—another storm would come—then you had to do the same thing over again.

They would shovel to the top of Smokey. Yes, indeed. I saw it shovelled as far as from Ingonish Ferry to the foot of Smokey. Every bit of it was shovelled and there was four feet put out of most of it. Yes.

There was a bunch from Ingonish started on the northern end—priest in Ingonish sent word up. Big storm came and they knew there would be no mail go for a week before you'd get the road open. So he sent a message up on a Sunday afternoon and he told me to get up on Smokey, start to open it, and that he'd send a bunch out from Ingonish. So we did. We started Monday morning about daylight and they started about daylight. There were more in their bunch—about 10 or 12 fellows. Tuesday evening it was just getting dark when we met on the top of Smokey, the barren there. We had the mail with us. They had horses with them and they took the mail back to Ingonish themselves and we turned back. Yes, oh, it was a hard grind.

(*Was there more snow then?*) I've seen it at Neil R.'s there and at Tommy MacDonald's when you'd be going across the road—the road was low then—and in the summertime you'd have to look up to see the house when you'd be going by there—and I saw in the wintertime going by there, you'd be looking down at them, and you could see them eating their meals at the table. Now I saw 25-foot poles—it's hard to believe but it's the truth—telegraph poles, and they weren't down in the hollow at all—they were put up in the side of the bank—and you could walk along them and the wires were right level with the snow. Yeah.

It was wicked down at Roddy Hector's there at Wreck Cove. They used to be all winter in the bank. It was wicked the way it would come. There was no woods up above the bank there and the snow would drift, boy, when the wind would come northwest after an easterly snowstorm. It'd pile that bank up as high as the house and Roddy would have to be there, boy, and if it was a stormy day it'd almost fill in as fast as they were shovelling it. Himself and Dan would be there, every morning, the first thing when they'd have their breakfast, about daylight, they'd have to go down there shovelling that bloody bank. And at Sandy MacDermid's—but it wasn't near as hard to keep it open—but it was wicked down there. And that French River was awful. We'd be shovelling there day and night.

(*After you delivered the mail, would you stay the night in Ingonish Ferry?*) Oh, no. Storm or no storm you'd have to try and make it home anyway. If you could get down you'd get back—but the next morning everything could be plugged up. You'd have to get them to turn out again shovelling. And the county wouldn't pay a cent to open it. (*Who paid the men who shovelled Smokey?*) I had to pay them. There was one time the county had a fellow on each side of Smokey, paying them so much a year for keeping the road open—but it was costing them too much so they cut that off altogether. I didn't have to pay much. I think around $2.50 a day. Of course, you could always get through along the shore here—the road was kept open voluntary. In the wintertime the people here used to put horses out after a snowstorm and open the road along—that was a big help. There were times when a storm would come and the roads would block up and you'd have to open them yourself, but as a rule the neighbours—the people along the route—were opening the road.

And then in the spring of the year when that snow would start melting, boy, after a rainstorm—you couldn't look at it. Horse would go out of sight in it. And you couldn't start with the car until the roads were dry—that'd be when the frost would come out—because it'd be all mud and you couldn't go through it at all.

The only thing you could do at Smokey was

get a boat. Go down with a boat when the ice would be out. I used to take the boat from Breton Cove here. I had five boats one time down in Ingonish—taking them down and leaving them down—the ice would come in and I couldn't get back. I'd have to leave the boat and walk back. Yes, walk back, over Smokey. And then when the ice would clear—a wind would come nor'west off the land again—the ice would push out a little. Well, I'd load another boat and take off with it to Ingonish. And maybe the wind would change in the meantime, when you were going down—coming from the east—and if it would, the ice was back in. And you'd just get around Smokey and get into Ingonish before the ice would catch you. Well, then you had to leave that boat and walk back.

Yes, I've had five of them down there. Motorboats that the fishermen had here. I had four down and I took another one down and the wind was off the land and the ice stayed out that day—so I tied them together and I got back with the whole business.

I took the mail six days a week. Every day but Sunday. And there were no holidays. Not even Christmas Day. When the weather was good I'd go to Englishtown and pick up the mail and take it all the way to Ingonish Ferry—and then come back home—every day. (*Did you deliver to each farm?*) Oh, no, you had post offices then: Jersey Cove, River Bennett, Indian Brook, Plaster, and Breton Cove; next was at Skir Dhu, Birch Plain, and Wreck Cove—and that was the last of them till you'd get to Byno MacIntyre's at Ingonish Ferry. (*And was there much mail?*) Well, you'd have the full of the car there; then you'd have to pile a lot of it on the outside, tie it on with a rope to take it all. Around Christmas you'd have an awful dose of it. There used to be an awful lot of Eaton's because it was the only way they had of getting clothes or anything. Merchants weren't keeping anything like that.

Aw, it was slavery at that time. There was nothing in it anyway, you know. I forget today what I was getting but what I had in the tender there was $2800 a year. (*And that would pay you and your brother and shovelling Smokey?*) Yes, and we used to keep around five horses. There was nothing in it. They thought I'd renew the contract, but I was fed up.

Danny MacAskill and the Ingonish mail

Fishing Smelts on the North River Ice

JACKIE SMITH: We fish with—"bag nets," they're called. The smelts are inside them and they're swimming around when you haul the net up. The smelt go with the tide and they'll swim, too. When there's hardly any tide, you'll see them swimming. Mostly they're sort of a lazy fish—let the tide carry them.

RAYMOND SMITH: It's set right in the current. And the smelts sometimes come backwards, sideways, headfirst. They're not all swimming.

JACKIE: The net is like a bag. The tide will open it up. Well, if there's no tide, it'll just hang straight down, the top part. Then when the tide comes, this top will then open up. And there's a funnel in it—only about two feet high by six feet long. And then once they go in through there, the net is a lot bigger and it's harder for them to find the opening to come back out.

RAYMOND: See, it's called a bag net, but it's halfway between a trap and a net.

JACKIE: One week you'll get good tides—you'll get a steadier flow of the water coming in. And the following week you'll get what they call "nip tides." They might run in maybe for ten minutes—all of a sudden stop and go back out. And

Jackie Smith

then run out maybe for half an hour and turn and come back in. You just set the net and you've got to be watching it continuously. If not, it'll go inside out on you. You've got to have the net set with the tide. They're like a big bag, so you have to have the tide in order to set the net.

RAYMOND: The new moon and the full moon—that's when we fish. We start three or four days before the new moon and fish till a couple of days after the moon, when the tides are at their best, running the best. If you went

low, the channel is the only water there is left. Then you can see it. If you come down here some day in the summertime, in the real low tide, you'll see the way the channel comes into the shore there, then out where we are—it goes out, almost to the middle, and there's another branch goes over to where Dan K. lived, and then the other one goes right up there by the point where Jackie is. **RAYMOND**: The tide goes right in here and raises it about four feet here, the water here. **JACKIE**: The fish follow along these channels. **RAYMOND**: They're feeding. They go up to feed on the flats. Towards the mouth of the river.

JACKIE: There's only about half a dozen nets on the river now [1985], every winter. There was one time there used to be all kinds of them there. Sometimes there'd be 13, 14, 15 lights—lanterns out on the ice—nets all along on both sides of the river. Oh, 25, 30 years ago. Day and night. Oh yes, they used to fish right around the clock, all day and all night. My father, when we

about fishing here and didn't pay any attention to the moon, you wouldn't get anything.

JACKIE: There's a channel in the North River, and you've got to set in the deep water in the channel. **RAYMOND**: And the trap has got to be set according to the turns in the channel. The channel's all curved. We generally set it on either the inside of the channel, where the fish are pushed to the outside. And then another turn you'd set it so you'd get them where they sweep in. The channel here is about 100 feet wide and it's about—right there where we're fishing—it's about 25 feet deep. But clear of the channel, there's only about three feet, four feet of water.

JACKIE: We have our marks on the trees on the shore so we know exactly where to put it every year.

DONNIE SMITH: We've been looking at it all our life. **RAYMOND**: Yeah, you can see the channel right clear. **DONNIE**: When the tide is dead

Donnie Smith

"Rolling the money out onto the ice."

used to live out West Tarbot—well, it was before I was born they lived out there. They had shacks along the river here—a lot bigger than this one. They used to have their bunks and everything in there. They took their own grub with them, and they used to stay there all week, fishing. And then there'd be a big truck from around; he'd collect all the fish from all the fishermen and take them over town and sell them. Take the money back to them.

DONNIE: Then when the tides were slack and that, they used to go visiting one another, from one shack to the next. **RAYMOND**: Telling stories and drinking tea. **DONNIE**: Little bit of rum. **RAYMOND**: When they'd get a spell of smelts, they'd probably get a bottle of rum.

JACKIE: They were making some extra money. Oh, yes. If they had a good run—a good winter with lots of smelts—they could make quite a few dollars. But they put in a lot of cold nights at it, too, for very little fish.

Raymond Smith

RAYMOND: First time I bought one [a net] I was about 14 years old. A friend of mine, a fellow I was going to school with, I borrowed the money from him. He signed a note in the bank in Baddeck for $50 for me. And in the first two years I fished, I never paid for it. I didn't get enough fish to pay back the $50. The old-timers were catching the smelts but the young fellows starting out weren't catching anything. That was 40 years ago!

Anybody starting out now would be in the same boat as I was. There could be all kinds of smelts there, and somebody come along and try to get them, he couldn't get them. Just picked it up from watching the old fellows. They just knew about the tides and understood the fish. (*What do you mean, "understood the fish"?*) Well, they come with the tides, they come in and out with the tide. If you make the least bit of noise, you won't get any. They're the spookiest fish of any fish. You make one big noise on the ice, and they're gone, you won't see them any more, maybe for a couple hours. You can't make a move. Just wait till they go in the trap, and then you haul it up and take them out. (*So that's why we walk ashore after you set the trap.*) Yeah. Well, there's fellows are out that don't know this! [Laughter.] (*You mean me. I guess I'd be two or three years paying for my trap, too!*)

JACKIE: They won't go in the net if you've got a light out there. **RAYMOND**: They'll stay around the light.

DONNIE: A few poor years, and then we started catching them. We often caught, now, some days, a couple of thousand pounds of smelts. In a day. That would be only an exception. We get a thousand dollars a ton for smelts now. We can sell all the smelts we can catch right now. About 50 cents a pound right now—that's from the fish buyers.

RAYMOND: Goldman in Glace Bay claims that these are the best smelts that he's ever handled. He handles all kinds of fish. And the North River smelts, he says, they're the best of all, by far, he says.

DONNIE: I don't know if we're at it for the money or not. Are we?

RAYMOND: I guess it's—I think it's—we've been working at it so long now, we don't want to give it up! [Laughter.] I believe people would think we're foolish, the last week, out here in this cold weather, coming fishing out here at five o'clock some mornings. You can't see the shore with snow.

DONNIE: You get tired sitting in the house knitting lobster heads. You've got to get outside.

JACKIE: There's lots of days when you're out there on the ice, you were wishing you were back.

RAYMOND: It's good fun, and it's good sport in it, too, when you go out like this—sitting in here nice and warm [in the fish shack], and then you go out and get two or three hundred pounds of smelts, like that. Then tomorrow, go over to Goldman's with them, and he'll pay you right there for them, and stop in the tavern coming home, and have steak and a beer.

JACKIE: Come back and set your net; hope you'll have to go the next day with another bunch.

RAYMOND: A lot better than going on unemployment. I'd rather be out there than be in Florida, now.

DONNIE: If you didn't enjoy it, you wouldn't be out there. That's what I say. If it was only for the money, you wouldn't bother with it.

RAYMOND: I may be down here smelting when I'm 90 years old!

Out on the ice in St. Ann's Bay, Donnie Smith said, "Listen. You can tell people about this. But don't tell them everything. If people knew what we have here, we wouldn't be able to afford the ground we're standing on."

An Orange in Chéticamp

MARIE (MRS. WILLIE D.) DEVEAU, *Belle Marche*: There was no paper in my time. I'm not too old. I'm 70. That's not too old. I bet that maybe the richest ones that lived down here maybe had the paper once in a while. There was nothing like the *Cape Breton Post*. The only paper we had was the *Dr. Chase Almanac*. We never used to have any Christmas cards. Maybe two or three cards. I remember my uncle sent me one. Well, look, I had that card in my clothes box for I don't know how many years.

And when we used to have oranges—it was so rare. I remember we used to go to picnics. Under tents at the church. My mother and my brother and me. Before we'd go in the picnic ground, we used to meet the orange papers. You know, the orange papers that were kind of gallivanting to the wind. And we used to jump on them and smell them and say, "Oooh, doesn't it smell good." But there were no oranges in them. We weren't without fruit, in season. But no oranges, no bananas, and no grapes. So, before we'd go home, Mama would say, "I'll buy an orange."

She bought an orange. We didn't peel it as we do today. I remember that so well. Mama made a hole in it. Then she kind of squeezed the orange, took a little, then she gave it to us. One after the other, we had each our turn. I used to squeeze and get the juice. My lips were so sore. Then I used to pass the orange to my brother. Okay, my brother had a suck for a while. Then he'd pass it back to me. We were walking from the church. We had that orange all the way home.

When we got home Mama would say, "Now, don't throw that orange away. I'm going to make you some drink with it." There was the peeling and the pulp. She used to cut it in little bits. Then she took that orange peeling and put it in a jar with water and sugar. She said, "Now, it won't be ready for 15 days or three weeks." But once in a while, I used to beg her to go with the spoon to taste if it was getting strong. Well, after a few days it was getting to have a good taste.

So, nothing was lost. We got that drink and what was left was no good at all. Mama said, "You better go throw it away." It was all soft, and it had given all its strength in the water. And we drank it. And it was good.

"Oh, my children! I am now more than 80 years old, and each time the southeast wind blows, I relive in my memory those terrible hours when, lost on the great moving field of ice, we could hear the sounding of our own death knell."—Hyacinthe Chiasson, one of three Acadian sealers from Chéticamp who were caught out on the ice in 1874. All three survived.

The *Aspy* in a Storm

THERE WERE ACTUALLY three *Aspy*s, each in turn—though to a steadily lessening degree—a main link for travel and goods between the island's commercial centre of Sydney/North Sydney and the small farming-fishing communities Down North. Several other coastal vessels served in this role all around Cape Breton. The second *Aspy* saw less work as the roads improved, and there was finally very little work for the third *Aspy* as the big trucks took over. She ended her days as a youth hostel near Halifax. "They stripped all the engines out of her and made one big hold. Oh, they had bands down there and bunks all over the place. She was a hard-looking sight then. And that was her last days." Dan K. Morrison worked aboard the first *Aspy* when the name *Aspy* still meant a welcomed vital contact to the wider world.

DANIEL K. MORRISON, *Wreck Cove*: The night before the big storm, a Tuesday night, we came back to White Point after going as far as Bay St. Lawrence. That day was a pretty day on the ocean, as calm as a pond. But at five o'clock Wednesday morning the captain woke up all the crew and both firemen to get the steam up and under way. He predicted that a storm was on its way. He said the storm glass was way down to the bottom. At that time, this was all he had to go by. There was no radio and no weather report.

So, we got the steam up, let the lines go, and away we went. Not long after, the wind came up and became so strong that if you went outside, you had to hold on to something or the wind would go with you.

The wind was coming up from the south. The *Aspy* didn't have much rigging on, but you couldn't hear anything with the wind whistling through those ropes. It was getting worse all the time, and the waves were swelling larger and larger. The engineer was strapped in his chair by the levers. He would shut off the steam of the engines when he felt the steamer plunging down since the propellers would lift out of the

Dan K. Morrison when he served on the *Aspy*

water. Sometimes he would miss, and you would think that the stern would shake to pieces with the propeller going a thousand times faster.

At last, the steamer wasn't going ahead one bit. I'm sure she was losing ground. When she would come down from a wave, the next one would bust down on her bow, hitting her with tons of water. You couldn't see anything but the forecastle mast. You would think sometimes she would never come up.

Just then, the whistle blew, and the captain told us to go around and tell the passengers to be on the watch since he was turning the *Aspy* around and heading back to White Point as soon as he would see a good lull. A good chance came, and we noticed she was turning. She was broadside when the first wave hit her and put her over on her side. I was holding onto one of the stringers for dear life since you couldn't stand on the deck because of the slant of the steamer. When the steamer started to come back I looked and saw how deep it was between the waves. I said to myself here she goes—and sure enough I knew she went so far on her side that if you were on the other side, you could have seen the keel. But, what saved her was the next wave would hit her broadside and put her far to the other side. Well, she finally came around and we were going before the waves.

We didn't take long getting back to White Point with the waves busting down on the *Aspy*'s stern all the way. White Point was a great shelter from storms coming up from the south, but a gale from the northeast would come right in there. Anyway, we tied the *Aspy* up with plenty of lines at a new government pier. The pier had three big spools to tie her to.

Around 11 o'clock, the wind shifted from south to southeast and then to east-northeast. The *Aspy* started rocking back and forth. Then the lines began snapping. There was a big coil of new rope in the locker room, and we got that out and put four new lines on her. No sooner had we done that than you could hear shot-like sounds of the lines breaking.

The captain came down and told us to get the steel hawser up from the aft storeroom. We had about eight fellows from White Point helping us. We always thought about how hard these men worked with us and without expecting any pay for their work. God bless them.

We put one end of the hawser out on the stern, tying it to the spool on the pier with ropes. We ran the other end of the hawser through the steamer and out on her bow. We were trying to secure the hawser at the bow as the storm was getting worse. The cable was so heavy we couldn't take up so much slack at a time. This one time, the undertow pulled the steamer out and yanked that big spool right out of the pier. The captain hollered to take the hawser in, and the White Point men had to come aboard to help

us. Then when they got a chance they jumped back to the pier. Captain Dan came down and told us we would have to go outside and anchor. He ordered us to get out both anchors to the last link of the chain.

Captain Dan MacDonald

We had another captain with us by the name of York who had replaced MacDonald when he had an operation during the summer. When MacDonald returned, York stayed on. He was a good, able man who was not afraid of anything, and that helped us a lot to keep our spirits up.

So, Dannie and Captain York went to get the anchors out after the *Aspy* was out quite a bit. They tied themselves with rope, and that saved them. A couple of times they had to jump into the rigging until the big waves passed by. One anchor had a very long chain on it, the chain on the other was shorter. Anyway, they both had a good hold on the bottom, and when the steamer would up on a wave, the chains would become so taut you'd think they'd pull the bow out.

We got out around two o'clock. I was staying up on the second deck, holding on. The wind was so strong, whipping the sea up like it was light snow. You couldn't see very far out on the ocean what with the spray. What frightened me was the big waves—sometimes in threes—would come together and break, then go some distance and break again. I said to myself if ever one of these comes down on the *Aspy*, she would never weather it.

The *Aspy* in a Storm

At last, I saw one of these waves coming right at us. You couldn't have timed it better as that wave busted right down on the bow. She was so slow coming back up that I thought she was sinking. As I looked down on the first deck, here the water was only a couple of feet below the second deck where I was. Captain Dan came out to see what had happened since they couldn't see through the spray on the windows. He said he thought for sure the housing, including the wheelhouse, was gone after the way the steamer had been shaken.

About 9:30 at night, another wave hit her and a lot of water poured down the stack, the deck, knocking out the dynamo and all the lights went out. The people in White Point watching the *Aspy*'s struggle thought for sure she had gone down. They sent a telegraph to the owners in Sydney that the *Aspy* was lost with all hands. After that, they couldn't get a message out to confirm it since trees fell across the wires, knocking out all communications.

The wind had shifted again to northwest and swung around to west, and what a wind it was, putting the steamer hard on her side. Talk about rolling. I was put on the 10 p.m. to 2 a.m. watch. Around midnight I knew she was dragging anchor, although it was hard to make anything out in the pitch darkness. At 1 a.m. I went to wake the captain, but he was already putting his coat on. He agreed that the steamer was dragging anchor, and told me to go and wake the rest of the crew. I went to York's cabin and rapped at the door, but there was no answer. I opened the door and had to laugh at what I saw. He had propped the mattress up against the side of the bed so he wouldn't roll or fall out. I had to shake him before he woke up.

So we weighed anchor. Captain Dan said with the west wind blowing this hard it would calm the sea and the waves down some, and he was right. We made for Ingonish. About 4:30 a.m. we arrived at the entrance to the harbour. However, the entrance is not very wide, and the lighthouse on Ingonish Beach had been swept away. The searchlights on the *Aspy* were little good in that gale, and the captain couldn't pick up the channel. So we had to back out and anchor again in the shelter of Middlehead. We had a nap and a good hot breakfast. Later, we came into the harbour, and soon a crowd gathered to find out how we weathered that awful storm down north.

The *Aspy* heading Down North

We left Ingonish around 10 o'clock in the morning with the wind blowing from the south. Mother and Father were pacing the floor waiting for some word on the fate of the *Aspy*. Father had been over to Alex J. Morrison's where they had the telegraph office, but the wires were still dead. They kept watching the ocean, and lo and behold the *Aspy* came into view, still battling the storm with white spray flying over her. The wind was coming from the south as it had the previous morning, causing the steamer to pitch in those waves while rolling in the waves stirred up by the northeaster. How glad we were as we steamed into Sydney Harbour. All the old-timers from the North Shore down to Dingwall said they had never seen a storm like it. Fishermen had never before seen a wind come up around full circle in 24 hours with no let-up.

I had my mind made up when I got my feet on solid ground that I would stay there. But then I read about the storm in the newspapers and how some big freighters for England had to turn back to Sydney for repairs with shattered pieces of lifeboats dangling from their davits. So I said to myself I must be a pretty poor sailor for quitting my job because of being in a storm. And I so much wanted to become a captain. I said to myself, If the *Aspy* was able to ride out that storm she'll ride out any storm. So I stayed on her until she tied up in January for the winter.

Malcolm Angus MacLeod, Birch Plain

Maisie Morrison, Wreck Cove

"Let Out the Cat!"
told by Evelyn Smith, Wreck Cove

THE STORY ABOUT THE CAT. Now that came from Donald Angus MacLeod from Lewis. I don't know if I told you how it came about. We were up in the Community Hall, four years ago this summer[1988]. And Donald Angus and his wife, and their daughter and her husband and their two children, were there. And we were having a ceilidh for them because they were going back to Scotland.

And I think Alice D. B. [MacLeod] told a story. And I had never been telling stories, up until that. And I think Alice told a little story. And maybe I told one. I can't remember. But anyway, he beckoned to me. He was sitting down near the back of the hall, and made a sign for me to come. And he whispered that story of the cat into my ear, in Gaelic. And he said—in Gaelic, he said to me, "I'm shy. I don't want to tell it. But I think it's funny. You tell it." And that's the first time that I told that story. And that came from Lewis, Scotland. And he's an elder in the

Free Church in Scotland, so when I tell the story, and I tell the source that it came from...! I don't think anyone thinks it's on the smutty side!

Storaidh a' chait

Bha Anna agus Mòrag a' fuireach ann an taigh beag snog 's na Hearadh. 'S e dithis pheathraichean a bh'unnta. Cha robh 'ad aosd idir, 's e nigheanan òg a bh'unnta, agus cha robh 'ad pòsda. Bha taigh beag snog aca, 's bha 'ad an comhnaidh ag iarraidh gum biodh a-huile dad 'na àite fhéin. Bha aon chat aca—cat boirionn. Agus cha robh 'ad a' leigeil an cat a mach, o là na dh' oichdhe, a shamhradh na gheamraidh. 'S tha mi cinnteach gu faod fhios a bhith agaibh gur son nach robh 'ad airson a' chat a leigeil a mach. Na leigeadh 'ad an cat a mach, bha feagal orra gum biodh piseagan aice, agus gun cuireadh na piseagan an taigh beag snog aca treimh' chéile.

Faodadh tu bhi cinnteach gu robh iomadach

The Story in English

(*Now, I'll make you tell me the story in English.*) Oh, in English. And I'm always afraid, when I'm telling the story—because sometimes I change the names of the sisters—and I think, "Is it Mòrag that left home, or is it Anna!" So I'm never sure. And I wouldn't like to make that mistake, but anyway.... (*It's just important that one of them gets out.*) Or, that the cat gets out! [Evelyn laughs.] But I'd like to add a little bit to that, that maybe the cat by that time has got so old that she doesn't care whether she goes out or not!

Anyway—Anna and Sarah were two sisters who lived in a little cottage by the side of the road in Harris, Scotland. They were young sisters, and they weren't married. They were very fussy housekeepers. They wanted everything to uair nuair a bha an cat glé neònach gu faigheadh i mach comh' ri na cait eile, nuair a thigeadh na cait firionn timcheall. Ach chan fhaigheadh i mach as a sud.

An ceann ùine, chaidh Mòrag an null gu, mar a chanadh sinn as a' Bheurla, gu'n a "mhainland" a' choimhead airson cosnadh. Agus fhuair i sin. Agus bha Anna aig an taigh leis a' chat. Cha robh fad's am bith gus na choinnich i gille òg, tapaidh. Agus thòisich a' suiridhe. Agus mar a thachras glé thric, an ceann ùine, rinn 'ad suas an inntinn gum pòsadh 'ad. Agus rinn 'ad sin. Agus dh'fhalbh 'ad air turus mar a ni chuid as motha do mhuinntir òg an deidh dhaibh pòsadh.

Agus bha Anna aig an taigh leatha fhéin, leis a' chat. Agus a h-uile là, bha i fuireach, a' feitheamh ach an tigeadh litir bho Mhòrag, ach ciamar a bha gnothaichean a' dol leatha. Bha là an deidh là a' dol seachad, 's cha robh guth a' tighinn. Ach a là seo, chunnaic i 'm post' a' tighinn, agus chuir e litir mór dhan a' mhailbox. A mach gun a ghabh Anna. Thuirt i rithe fhéin, "Oh, gheibh mi naidheachd a nisd ach ciamar a tha Mòrag a' faighinn air adhart."

Thug i a' litir a stigh 's riab i fosgailt' e. Ach an deidh fhosgladh, nuair a sheall i, cha robh sgread air a' sgriobhadh as a' litir, ach na ceithir facail seo:

"Leig a-mach an cat!"

be just so in their little cottage. They had one cat, a female cat. And they didn't allow the cat to go out, day or night, winter or summer. And I think you know the reason why. They were afraid if the cat went out, that she would become pregnant. And if you get a few kittens around in your house, they can upset things, and they didn't want that.

So the poor cat wasn't allowed to go out. And I'm quite sure that there were many times, when the male cats would come calling, when the cat would be very happy if she could have gone out.

After a period of time, Sarah went over to, as we say, the mainland, to look for work. And she did get work there after a while. And things were going well. And Anna was home alone with the cat. And as happens quite often, after a while Sarah met up with a nice young man, and they started courting. And after a while, they decided that they'd get married. Which they did. And they went on their honeymoon.

And Anna was left home, waiting each day patiently, wondering if there would be a letter come from Sarah, and as to how she was getting along on her honeymoon.

Days went by and the mail would come, and there was no letter. But finally this day she saw the mailman stopping at the mailbox, and he put a large envelope into the box. And she ran out, and she thought, "Oh, I'm going to get news from Sarah now as to how everything is going on her honeymoon."

She ran into the house and she ripped open the envelope. But when she looked on the sheet inside the envelope, there was nothing written on it, but in big bold letters, these four words:

"Let out the cat!"

Our thanks to Catriona Nic Tomhair Parsons, a noted instructor in the Gaelic language, for transcribing the Gaelic.

Cape Smoky on the Old Cabot Trail

CAPE SMOKY - CABOT TRAIL · CAPE BRETON

On the Old Cabot Trail

A Fox on North Mountain

CLARENCE BARRETT, *Middle River*: One evening on North Mountain I was sitting at the edge of the bank overlooking the ravine on the Grande Anse side of the mountain. There are no lookoffs on that side of the mountain, unfortunately, and the shoulder of the road is not wide enough to park on. But you can walk, stopping to enjoy the view whenever you want. As you walk further up the road from the Lone Shieling, you can look down with a bird's-eye view onto the forest of sugar maples cradled in the valley below. The valley beside you narrows into a ravine as you ascend the hill, and the steep slopes across the chasm side draw closer and closer.

At a bluff overlooking the ravine I stepped over the guardrail and sat down with my back against one of its posts. The valley was still—just a murmur from the stream hidden in the bottom of the ravine and a couple of thrushes singing from somewhere in the hills. To the west the valley stretched away towards the village of Pleasant Bay. The smell of the sea wafted up the valley and a low bank of fog moved in from the gulf to blanket the village. The sun was painting the hillsides in subtle shades of mauve and other colours I don't even know if there are names for.

After I'd sat there awhile I noticed a fox coming up the road. He appeared to be hunting, occasionally weaving in and out among the guardrail posts to check the grass for something or other. I just sat there, watching. He didn't seem to be in any hurry; who would be on such an evening? I was on the ravine side of the guardrail when he finally came abreast of me on the pavement. He trotted by me a few paces and, getting my scent, stopped as if he had run into an invisible wall. He turned, saw me, stood there for a moment, then sat down at the edge of the pavement, watching me with eyes half closed. He yawned. I yawned. I thought he was going to fall asleep. After a while he got up, slipped under the railing, stepped to the edge of the ravine as if admiring the view, and nonchalantly sat down an arm's length away. For about five minutes we both sat there, gazing out over the ravine, sharing the quiet scene surrounding us. Then he casually got up, stretched, went back under the railing and kept going up the road.

Foxes have a reputation for pilfering. One item they seem to covet is golf balls, and they have been known to complicate a golfer's score-keeping by dashing onto a green and disappearing with his ball. One day some people showed up at a Park Visitor Centre inquiring where the fox den was located at the MacIntosh Brook campground. Since the Park doesn't keep a registry of fox dwellings, the staff weren't able to help him. Still, the visitors persisted. The attendant wondered why they wanted to know the whereabouts of the den. Pointing to his stockinged feet, one of the visitors replied, "Because he's got our shoes!" The unsuspecting campers had left their shoes on a picnic table overnight and a fox had run off with them.

"We made it at the cost of a blown tire, a nosebleed from the dust, a few dents in the chassis, a damaged spring, a cramp in my back, and sore shoulders from working the steering wheel."—author Hugh MacLennan, 1939

Bill Fraser Walks the Cabot Trail

WORD WAS ALWAYS GETTING OUT that moonshine was being manufactured in Meat Cove. [This would be in the 1930s.] I got a call from Bay St. Lawrence, from Fr. Paul MacNeil, the parish priest. He would send me a message in Latin, and I'd be able to decipher it. That's the only way we could do it, because everybody could read Morse code up and down the Shore, and if he didn't send it in Latin, they would have known what we were doing. I remember the old telegraph operator in North Ingonish; he used to get cross when you'd get a message in Latin.

I was there a couple of years when this happened. So I decided, well, something's got to be done about this, and the only time you can do anything about it, really, is to go in the wintertime. In the summertime nobody would give you information.

So, now listen to this. I decided this winter that I would go to Meat Cove and try to catch this man with moonshine, and get his still, if I could. And I went on my skis from Ingonish, down through Neil's Harbour, stopped at New Haven, just past Neil's Harbour, and had a bit of a lunch at Mrs. Budge's place. She saw me going past, came to the door and called me in. And I can still remember, because she did something I never saw done before—she was frying me an egg on the stove, and she put a saucer— just a plain saucer from under a cup—on the stove, and a little butter in it, and put the egg on it, and that's how she fried the egg. I never saw that done before.

But I had lunch there, and went over where the White Point road is now, walked over there on skis. Crossed that long beach into Dingwall, went to the hotel and had supper there that evening, and it was the usual—you always had corned beef hash at the hotel, particularly in

Bill Fraser, Superintendent R.C.M.P., Rtd., Baddeck

the wintertime. There was no fresh meat around. And I had supper there at five o'clock, and then I got on my skis and went another 12 miles across the beach and into Bay St. Lawrence, or St. Margaret's, to the parish house, the glebe house, Fr. Paul.

Had a cup of tea with Fr. Paul and talked with him until 11 o'clock. He went to bed, and I got on my skis again, and I went from there to Meat Cove in the middle of the night on skis. Packed the skis up after I got down into Meat Cove—the first hill—and then started hunting for tracks into the woods. And lucky enough, I found a track into the woods and I followed it. And I was back quite a distance back of Meat Cove, and I came upon a little camp. There were four dogs tied there. There were barrels of mash sunk in the snow, in the ground, and the fireplace was set up, and the still was set up there. So I tasted the mash—I'd learned to do it in Inverness County—and realized that pretty soon they were going to have to run this off. So I picked myself out a nice tree to lean against, across a little brook.

I was only there about an hour when I heard somebody coming—it was a man coming. He fed the dogs, and then got the fire going, and started to run the moonshine. When he got a little bit run off, he took a sip of it and kind of smacked his lips. I waited till he got a little bit more in the can, and then I jumped him. Saved the moonshine and smashed up the still, put the fire out, broke the barrels, cut the dogs loose, and said, "Well, I'll be back and get you. I've got to send this away for analysis." Got on my skis again and went back to Ingonish.

Sent the stuff out in the mail. Eventually it came back, after a month or so, and I went back up to Meat Cove. I went to Cape North on snowshoes. And I hired a horse in Cape North to take me to Meat Cove to bring this prisoner out. We arrested the guy. It was in Inverness County rather than Victoria. I put him in the sled, and stopped at MacGregor's at the foot of Cape North Mountain for the night. I had an extra pair of snowshoes for him. Got him up early in the morning, and we had breakfast, and we started out to snowshoe to Pleasant Bay and Chéticamp.

At Pleasant Bay we had to stop and have the trial before the magistrate there. He was convicted, of course, and sentenced to the county jail at Port Hood. We went on, climbed up MacKenzie Mountain, got across the top. Then my prisoner played out on me—he couldn't go any further. Nothing I could do. I knew he couldn't run away on me. I said, "Well, you come as slowly as you can, or sit down and rest here, and I'll go on down ahead into Cap Rouge. I'll get someone to come with a handsled and get

you." Which I did. Christopher Aucoin and some man came up—I don't know who it was. But it was Christopher Aucoin was the first house in Cap Rouge. And he went back up the French Mountain and picked up this prisoner and brought him down. Then I took him to Chéticamp and put him in jail for the night at the cell of the detachment. Went to the hotel.

The next morning he was so hard used up that he could hardly walk. So I had to hire a man with a horse and sleigh, and start for Inverness. I put him in the seat with the driver, and I jumped on the back of the sleigh, and I ran and jumped off and ran again, and we made Inverness that night. That's another 47 miles from Chéticamp. I put him in jail overnight, and then got up early in the morning and took him on the passenger train to Port Hood, put him in jail and gave him warmth, and that was fine. Came back to the station and caught the freight train at 11 o'clock. It got to Point Tupper, and then I caught the evening train into Sydney. I went into Sydney and stayed there the next day, all day the next day.

And then the following morning, two of the fellows drove me out to Big Bras d'Or—it was frozen—the ferry wasn't running. I had my pack on my back and two pair of snowshoes. And I got a long pole, and I started walking across Big Bras d'Or to the ferry [wharf] at New Campbellton. And the ice broke under me, and I went in and got wet. But I had my pole, and I got out. They were watching me from the shore. I got out and I walked to shore.

When I got ashore, I put on my snowshoes, and I snowshoed 54 miles to Ingonish that day, getting home at about 10:30 at night.

A woman at the foot of Smokey, on the North Shore side of Smokey, coaxed me to stay there in the evening. I stopped in there and had a bit to eat, and waited till about eight o'clock and had a bit of a rest. And then got on my snowshoes and went up Smokey. Actually, literally, and I can remember—it was a lovely winter's night—I actually jogged down on snowshoes, going down the other side of Smokey. Crossed over the Ingonish Ferry along the shore, and got home in North Ingonish at 10:30 p.m.. Snowshoeing 54 miles that day. It didn't bother me one single bit.

I got up the next morning at eight o'clock, down in the office making out reports.

That's just one incident there. I had another incident going the other way. A couple of years later, or a year and a half later—I had four prisoners in the jail. And it came that I couldn't keep them any longer, and to try to get to Baddeck with them. So, I had them all lined up, and I went and I hired three teams of horses. And I put two prisoners in the first horse and team, and one in the next horse and team, and another team behind with myself and a prisoner. So the middle team had one prisoner, but they'd change back and forth so they'd ease off on those two horses. And we started from Ingonish early in the morning—it was way long before seven we got out of there. And that's a long drive to Baddeck.

Came down over Smokey, up the North Shore, stopped at D. B. MacLeod's and had lunch, fed the horses, and then came on from there, crossed the ferry, and came up to Rocky Side. Came to St. Ann's, and stopped at the MacLeods' at St. Ann's, put the horses in the barn—I can remember it so well. I wired ahead

that I'd be there, and asked them to have lunch for these prisoners. Put the horses in the barn, rubbed them down, took the harness off, put the blankets on them, and I gave each horse a pail of lukewarm water, sprinkled with a good share of oatmeal in it, and then a feed of hay, and a little bit of oats after that. Stayed there till about half past eight. Let the horses have a rest particularly, not so much us. Hitched them up again and came to Baddeck and put the prisoners in jail. I don't know of any other time, really, you could take horses sixty miles and come over Smokey, a hill like Smokey. But it was necessity, and the horses had a good rest at noon, and they had a good rest in the evening. And they were none the worse for it. I let them stay in the barn for two days while I stayed in Baddeck, till they rested up, and then I went back home with the three teams. That was just two expeditions out of Ingonish.

Père Anselme Chiasson, Chéticamp

Trap-Fishing Mackerel with Mike MacDougall

MIKE MACDOUGALL, *Ingonish Beach*: To get ready for mackerel season, it's almost a year-round job. You'll put your stuff away the last of August and then come January or at least February, you start thinking about mending the nets. Then when the weather gets fine—probably the last week of April to the 15th of May—you can paint and caulk your boats. You want to be ready to set your twine [the trap] by the 24th of May. This year [1977] was supposed to be a late spring. It wasn't. The drift ice stayed around till just about lobster fishing time [May 15] but I'm sure there were mackerel missed here. They figured the mackerel would be late because of the drift ice, but they were here about the 27th or 28th of May. You can count on their coming. You hear that they're getting them in Hubbards and Lunenburg—then Petit-de-Grat and L'Ardoise.

Within the next two days after L'Ardoise, you're going to get mackerel here. Definitely. You're not going to get a big catch. You'll start probably with two or three. They call them the leaders. Next thing you know you're in the thousands.

Good mackerel fishing—25,000 pounds would be a small day. That's a man with two fish traps. Two fish traps for the first two weeks, if things go right and you get the right kind of weather and wind, you could easily land 100,000. I've had in three days 101,000 on Monday, 105,000 on Tuesday, and 109,000 on Wednesday for a total of 315,000 pounds for three days. The biggest catch of fish that ever was weighed in this harbour in mackerel—I can't go back to the days of haddock—I had it in 1974. I had 114,985 pounds—one day. In 1970, which was the crack year, I had 1,035,000 pounds of fish for the month of June to the 15th of July. We had two traps in the water. We had two collecting boats—good service—but the two boats couldn't handle what we were taking out of the two traps. They could just look after one. The other trap below was loaded every morning and every evening with fish—and we just had to let her sit there most of the season.

Red Dan Smith mends a net on the shore at Jersey Cove

MIKE MACDOUGALL: The one man who I have to thank, who is responsible for this for me—is Dan Smith of Jersey Cove. Red Dan Smith. In my travelling and time he was one of the finest gentlemen I ever met. He fished years and years—all his life. And he came down here and he got me interested and he got me on the road. He stuck by me and told me everything possible that I know about it—and he was a hard man to fool on anything. He was an expert on twine, in putting nets together. In my first year, Dan came out with us, set the main anchor. He set that trap to show us the picture of it, back of Smokey. Then we got in trouble, through me, because I had her on the bottom and she hooked and

tore and I had 10 days with Dan there with me, trying to get her back in the water. I couldn't even mend a mesh of twine. But he told me, "Fellow, if you're going to get into this racket, you've got to learn it." So I went at it and now I can just about do anything around twine. And I did everything on my own ever after.

Red Dan and Mary Smith

Donovans and Doucettes and the Clyburn Valley

Today, the Clyburn Valley is the world-famous 18-hole Highlands Links golf course, as well as a splendid place for hiking and cross-country skiing—part of the Cape Breton Highlands National Park. Although most of the pioneer settlers had left the valley around the turn of the 20th century, the fertile land continued as pasture land for cattle. Local history tells of 17th-century mining. Then there was a brief flurry of gold fever that brought people to the Valley in the early 20th century. Remnants of that enterprise still survive.

Only two families lived in the Clyburn Valley when the National Park took over in 1936: the Doucettes and the Donovans. Neither family had many years before the park closed the valley to human habitation.

MAURICE DONOVAN: We lived in the Clyburn Valley. We got a son called Clyburn. He was born up there, and we called him Clyburn. And if we had of stayed, and had another girl, I'd have called her Franey [after the peak overlooking the Valley]. **EMMA DONOVAN**: Oh, my father thought that was the worst name in the world. He near had a fit, being we called the baby Clyburn. **MAURICE**: Called after the river, and the river is called after the first white settler that settled in Ingonish.

(*Where was your house when you lived up the Clyburn?*) On Number 9. (*That's the golf course today.*) **EMMA**: There's an apple tree there. Right where the house was. **MAURICE**: At that time the river, the Clyburn River, was teeming with trout and salmon. I counted 129 salmon one evening there in that pool, just looking down from the rocks at them. The trout—our kids used to catch more trout—they were there all the time fishing.

EMMA: We had no water in the house. We had to go down the hill to get it from the brook.

Tom & Lucy Doucette's home in the Clyburn Valley, 1939—now Number 11, Cape Breton Highlands Links

One morning I guess there was too much water used—what the kids used in the nighttime—so I said, "Charlotte, you run down and get some water for breakfast," or before they go to school or something. Maurice had to rig up and go and hunt for her, for she had a rod hid down by the brook. She was down there and she had nine trout when he got down. **MAURICE**: She was shivering, but still fishing.

EMMA: But you'd think the children would hate the valley, for they were scared to go out at night, frightened of the bears. But when they left that valley…they all—I don't know what type of harness Maurice put on a cow and a calf—and they all had to go over the mountain—there was a pathway. We kept on right up to the head of the harbour—every one of those children going with an animal apiece and crying because they had to leave the valley.

MAURICE: We haven't been up there since a long time. **EMMA**: I said I'd never go back in after. **MAURICE**: She hates to go back in and look at the old place up there. We were kind of like pioneers there.

They drove me out of there. And do you know how much money I got then for it? $1,500. [For] 64 acres.

That MacDonald farm across the river, those beautiful orchards there. My grandfather imported all those trees. Lots of apples. **EMMA**: There used to be a lot of rhubarb, strawberries, and all kinds of stuff there.

MAURICE: My mother killed a bear up there over in that place. It was blueberry time and they were picking blueberries for preserving. And they had a big porch on their house, and they'd put the kitchen stove out there in the spring so it wouldn't be too hot in the house. That's where they were stewing the blueberries down—out on this porch—and they left the window out that night. They always kept an axe in the house, took it in at night, case they needed it. They heard a racket through the night, and my mother and Aunt Liz came down. Aunt Liz had the lamp and my mother had the double-bit axe, and when they opened the door, the bear came in with a kitten in his mouth. He had picked the kitten up where it was sleeping on the porch, and he was going toward the window. And my mother swung the axe and cut the backbone off him and killed him. The bears are more plentiful now.

TOM DOUCETTE: My grandfather, John Doucette, settled in Ingonish. He married Jane Brewer from North Ingonish and they settled in the Clyburn Valley, about where the 9th green of the golf course is now. Their house was built on a sort of a small foothill at the foot of the mountain on the south side. Jane Brewer/John Doucette had quite a large family: the oldest being James, then there was Margaret, Annie, Frank, Bill, and a daughter by the name of Mary, and finally John, and my father whose name was Tom.

LEONA DOUCETTE DUNPHY [Tom's sister]: The Doucette tract [of land], now, that would be my great-great-grandfather. But he owned that tract of land—I forget how many acres—this one had 58 acres in the original grant. It started over—you know where the Esso service station is—and it went over and included where the park entrance is, and it went back over the mountain and included [part of] the Clyburn Valley. So my great-grandfather left the Clyburn lot of land to my grandfather—that would be John Doucette—and that took in—well, the only piece that was left then that would be still in possession of the Doucette family would be the piece of land this side of the swinging bridge [over the Clyburn River].

And when my grandfather left and moved to New Waterford—that would be probably back at the turn of the century—well, it was shortly after my father [Thomas Leo] was born, and he was born in 1897. They moved up to New Waterford or Dominion somewhere, and the piece of land lay vacant all those years.

So, he had willed that to my father. My father had been overseas. He had gone when he was 17, and he came back in 1919 with his English bride and a small child, and they settled in New Waterford. And you know, it was pretty hard scraping. Anyway, they settled in New Waterford and he went back to mining. He had been in the mines when he was 13 years old. He had suffered a lot in the war. He had been wounded in the arm and shoulder, and he just couldn't take that type of work. It wasn't what he wanted anyway, so he eventually talked my mother into moving down and settling at the Clyburn.

I wasn't born. They came back in 1929 or 1930. When they first came back there was no house on that property. He [Father] decided he'd build a log cabin on that Clyburn property. So in March of 1930—he used to go up the Clyburn—he'd snowshoe up in winter. And he used to cut logs and put them in the river and keep them moving down, and when they'd jam up, he'd go in the river—take his clothes off and go in the river—and clear the jam. (*He must have been a big, strong man.*) He wasn't a big, strong man. He was determined—probably that's the word for it. He was very, very determined.

So anyway, he got the logs down far enough to build a cabin on that piece of land. And I was born in March of '31, and in May of '31 we moved into the log cabin. I don't recall the log cabin, but I remember it afterwards 'cause he used it as sort of a little barn for chickens and whatnot. So he had built the house—the foundation is still there—just below the swinging bridge, just off to one side of the golf course.

You'd see it in the summertime. It's probably grown up with weeds and everything. But he had a beautiful flower garden. He had bleeding-heart and he had everything—in front of the house.

TOM DOUCETTE: They had moved to Ingonish from New Waterford, with the intention of moving to the Clyburn. Well, of course the Depression had just been on a year. And my mother and father came down in April. And the old homestead was still standing in the Clyburn [Valley].

And the night we left Sydney to come down on the *Aspy* to Ingonish, there was a heck of a thunder-and-lightning storm. And when we arrived the next day—it was a nice day, beautiful day. We arrived on the *Aspy*. All our furniture, old Captain Peters stored it in the *Aspy* shed. And we walked up to my Uncle Jim Doucette's, who had the house across from where the Mountie police headquarters is now.

We stayed there for a couple of hours. And then we walked over to the Clyburn, and walked up through what was then just a bush road, all grown over. And we got there in the evening. And we found the house had burned down the night before in a thunder-and-lightning storm. And there were just smouldering timbers left. So we spent the night in the ferns—my father

made a lean-to. That was my mother, my father, and five children. The youngest was about three.

And in the morning we got up, and…I might get emotional…. So anyway, if you can imagine: a small boy waking up to a paradise. The river's there; but the house is gone. So old Jimmy Donovan—that's Sadie's grandfather—came up looking for a cow, and he saw some smoke. So he came over. And he took us down to the mouth of the Clyburn where he had a cabin. And we spent about a month there. And then my father rented Simon Brewer's house [in Ingonish].

Anyway, we moved in there. It was all alders. My father cleared it out, and I think he was paying five dollars a month rent for it, at that time. There was no money in Ingonish—that was Depression days. The plaster mines had closed a year and a half before. And they cleared the land, and about two acres. And he did some gardening there—he was a good gardener—potatoes and stuff. And he bought a fishing boat. Which didn't work out. But I mean, he always traded potatoes and cabbage for fish. And he had his pension, and I guess at that time you'd say we were about the most well-off, in Ingonish.

But anyway, a year and a half later they decided to build [the log cabin Leona spoke of] up on the Clyburn—him and Simon Brewer and a couple of other fellows. Cut down the logs, and they built a cabin, 24 by 20. And made three rooms in it. Dirt floor. And chinked all with moss and everything. And we lived quite comfortable there for about two years.

And that brought it up to 1935. And then my father cut down a lot of heavy timber, and had them sawed up in the mill over at North Ingonish. And he built a six-room house. And then the log cabin was taken down, and all the logs were sawed up to build a two-story barn.

But then, National Park started [1936]. And, I think [my parents] had the idea that the four older ones—well, six by then—should get a better schooling up around New Waterford. So they decided to move [back to New Waterford].

LEONA DUNPHY: You jump from 1935 to moving back to New Waterford. It was the life

Maurice & Emma Donovan's house, 1939.
Golfers on today's 9th hole of Cape Breton
Highlands Links golf course, 1941.

we had [in the Clyburn Valley]—those years in between—it was paradise. It was paradise. And I mean, we were so poor that it was....

TOM: There were no fishing regulations, really. You were allowed to catch 20 trout a person. And you could go out before breakfast and you could come back with 10 big trout like that. (*That's a foot and a half.*) Well, I caught one that was 18 inches long, on the 17th of May, 1936. And we used to climb up at Young's Pool and MacNeil Pool—the trees came out over the water—and we'd climb up a tree there and see who could count the most salmon. They were in like logs. In the Clyburn. **LEONA**: In the pool.

But life up there, it was—like, where the golf course is now—we lived just below the swinging bridge. **TOM**: The 9th Green. **LEONA**: And it was back in under the mountain, in the lee of the mountain, where the house was. Our father had that all planted. And every one of us worked in that garden, weeding. **TOM**: That was intervale land. You'd go down that deep and wouldn't get a stone...all pure leaf mould.

LEONA: Oh, Dad had a big farm—he was one of the fortunate ones because he had—he was getting a disability pension from the government for his war service. In the '30s—late '20s, early '30s—he was getting $40 a month, which more than bought the staples. You know: flour and milk and butter. And he had acres and acres of turnips and carrots and cabbage and cauliflower—everything—and he used to ship it out to the Cosmopolitan Stores in Sydney [on the *Aspy*], and he'd get a credit voucher for whatever the value of that amount of produce was. And probably before the last trip—maybe the second-last trip of the *Aspy*—he'd mail in his list of staples he thought he'd need for the winter. And they'd come back—the Cosmopolitan Store would ship them back on the second or last trip of the *Aspy*, and we'd be well stocked then for the winter. Along with that, he'd stock up all the vegetables he needed for himself, and my mother used to bottle a lot. Once they got their own in, and what was left, I remember going over to North Ingonish and the Centre in the horse and wagon selling vegetables. All the surplus was sold door-to-door.

TOM: And he got his fish [that way]. And of course, you didn't have to worry too much about meat. There was lots of deer around and no game wardens. And the Mounties didn't bother you too much if you took one out of season. And rabbits, partridge.... And he took a salmon out of there [in 1936] that was 56 inches long. It'd been up in the river all winter. And it got high and dry when the water went down—small pool— remember the big salmon he got in the ice?

LEONA: Yeah. I remember the one he lost because of me, too! Wherever he went, I was with him—it didn't matter where, I had to be there. Well, he had this big salmon on the hook and he said, "Leona, go back to the house and get my dip net." I'd go a little distance towards the house and the salmon would splash and I'd run back: "Did you lose him, Papa?" He'd say, "No. Go to the house and get my dip net." And I'd get a little distance again and the salmon would jump again and I would run back: "Did you lose him, Papa?" So this happened maybe half a dozen times, and finally I went back and he said, "Never mind. I don't need the dip net—I've lost him."

(*We keep using this word "paradise." But didn't you feel cut off from the world?*) **TOM**: No. Never thought of it. **LEONA**: I never knew there was a world, outside of that. **TOM**: You just saw that circle with a dome over it, and that was your world. **LEONA**: But I can tell you this, that there hasn't been a week gone by since we left there that I haven't missed it. Because life was just altogether different after we moved to New Waterford. It wasn't the same at all, from the life we had lived up there. It just seems that the years I spent up there, I was always a child. And then all of a sudden, you know. When we left there, the war broke out, and you had to grow up so.

I still think it's a wonderful life for young people. I think it's a wonderful way for kids to start to grow up, is in that kind of an environment. Because you don't get spoiled, that you want everything you see, you know, because—what you get, you don't see that much, so you don't, you know. And you learn to earn what you can.

TOM: When I say a paradise: you had everything you wanted. The only thing you had to buy was coal, oil, sugar, and tea, practically. And you could live without that, if you didn't have it.

LEONA: That valley flooded every spring.

It was ideal for farming conditions—floods in the spring, and when that dries out, you're a little later planting, but there's no disadvantage to that, because the ground is warm enough that the seeds germinate faster. We always had a beautiful garden. He used to start all his transplants—like cabbage, cauliflower, and everything like that—in the house in flats, and he'd transplant them.

(*Maurice, why did you take your family out to the Clyburn in the first place?*) **MAURICE DONOVAN**: Well, it was nice farmland there. And we need to farm to live.... Before [going out the Clyburn] I was in the preventive service—federal government—chasing the rumrunners.

EMMA: When Maurice decided to move to the Clyburn, he had to take the house down in sections, and take it up onto a horse and wagon, and take it up the Clyburn Valley. Well, we didn't live up there that many years until our land was taken from us by the park.

That beautiful soil that was up there. You didn't need fertilizer or anything, everything grew. There were no weeds into it or anything. Beautiful, beautiful brook, stream, running down that Clyburn. It was just nothing but beauty. **MAURICE**: Then the government came in and took it over for the national park. **EMMA**: For very little. **MAURICE**: Supposedly expropriation. I told one of the fellows, I said, "You've got the wrong name on it." I said, "'Slavery' is the best way to put that there—this is not expropriation."

EMMA: We didn't want a park at our property. And I don't think that anybody that lost their property wanted a park at their property. I know Maurice fought for his. He even went out and stood with a gun when they came up to come in on his property that morning—the head fellow that brought his crew and came up. And Maurice stood with a gun. He warned him, "Don't come one foot on my property." And I had been down below where the cattle were. I was down there. So...Mr. Stewart came up the road a piece and cut down...where the barren was. And he came down, he asked me, he said,

"Emma, go on up," he said, "and talk to your husband. Tell him to go in and put the gun away." He said, "It's going to go anyhow, and it's no good for him to try and fight it." So he made all kind of promises that Maurice'd never be without work while he was able to work, or any of his sons—they'd always have work. And all those promises were made to him—"Go ahead and let us have your property."

It was heartbreaking. It was, you know, such beautiful soil. And the beautiful forests of wood and everything we had. And the kids enjoyed the fishing, you know, there, and everything. (*And how many years were you there before this happened to you?*) About three years. (*You had put your house back together.*) Oh, yes. MAURICE: House and barn. EMMA: Nothing for that. Nothing for the house or barn. You could take it or you could leave it.

(*You're standing there with that gun that day. And did Emma come and talk to you?*) MAURICE: Yeah. (*And what did you decide?*) I decided I'd better not shoot somebody. I went in and put the gun away. EMMA: He'd have never shot anybody, that's for sure. But he thought he'd scare them.

MAURICE: Before they came in there on Monday morning—on Sunday afternoon I was out to church, and I went over to the hotel there…. It's the Island Inn now. That wasn't the name that was on it then. But anyhow, there's where they were boarding, the fellows that came in to build the golf course. So I went over there, and the superintendent of the building job was Bill Stewart from British Columbia. He and a couple more of his men that's with him. I went in and I told him—he was up on the verandah. I just went to the edge of the verandah and I told him, I said, "Now, I'd like to warn you before Monday morning, not to cross my property, or to put your men there." I said, "If you do, you'll have a job for the undertaker." And he jumped off of the verandah—oh, he could have killed me right there. I wasn't long coming out of my coat. I said, "Come on." I said, "And if you go down, you'll never get up." He wouldn't—he was a way

bigger man than I was. He backed away.

But after he got finished with me [after expropriation], he said, "Look, I took more liking to you last Sunday," he said, "for standing on your feet and challenging a man the size of me." I said, "Yes, and I know I can beat you, too!"

(*When you say they came out with their crew, what did they intend to do that day?*) They were going to start working on my part of the property. Golf course—there's two holes and two fairways in the property that I owned there. Nine and Ten. Now, I had my crop in—potatoes and garden and everything—down in, where Number 10 Green is at now, all that part there. They bulldozed that away, and never got five cents for it. You know, it was a terrible hard living up until then. And it was Angus L.'s government was in in Halifax, and I've been a bitter Tory ever since.

Fifteen hundred dollars. Nobody in the country here considered it a fair price, no. They asked me before the price ever was set on it—their lawyer from Sydney—Smith MacIvor was his name. He came in and he told me what they were going to give. He asked me first, he said, "How much will you be satisfied to settle for, to leave here?" "Well," I said, "I've been thinking about this since…." I said, "I'll leave for fifty thousand dollars." And I said, "I think you'll be getting a bargain at that." "Well," he said, "the price that they're offering you is fifteen hundred."

They said, "We don't want your house, and we don't want your barn—we're not paying for that at all. If you leave it there, we'll put the torch to it. If you take it away and make use of it, that's all right with us." That's the words they gave me.

Of all the people that lost their land here, to the national park, I'm the only living one that's left. I stayed till they buried them all. EMMA: That'd have been a good picture to take. We had six children. The two smallest ones couldn't—but every one of them had a rope on an animal—a cow or a calf or something—going over the shortcut over the mountain, from the Valley where we lived. Went over the mountain and came out down there somewheres around

where the Senior Citizens' is—it came out there. And then went on up the road then to the other farm we were going to. Would have been a picture to take, like you were getting driven out, eh? Everybody going with an animal. **MAURICE**: It reminded me right there that day of the Expulsion of the Acadians. I saw those in pictures, of the women leading cattle when they left. This was the Expulsion of the Irish this time. (*Out of the Clyburn Valley.*)

EMMA: Oh, we loved it, and the kids loved it. That was the beautiful part about it. In fact, when they were leaving, you could hear them crying and me telling them not to cry. They were crying because they had to leave.

LEONA DUNPHY: I believe it was probably isolation that drove my grandfather out of here [at the turn of the century]. The piece of land he left was never lived on again until my dad came back. The next birth after my father's birth was the twins, and it's quite unusual when you think of it, because his great-great-grandmother died up there giving birth to triplets—and her and the three babies were buried together. They all died.

(*About the twins....*) My mother was due to give birth in May '37. They were born on March 24, 1937, and my mother never recovered until late in May. It was then my father made his decision to leave the Valley.

Dad was born up there in 1897. And there were no more children born there until the twins were born in 1937.

TOM DOUCETTE: The Clyburn remained empty all that time. You see, the gold mine closed in 1896. And that finished the Clyburn. Most people moved out of it. And there were a few people still hung onto their land, like old Johnny Hines. **LEONA**: They kept cattle out there. **TOM**: They used it for pasturage, and that's all. And we moved in there in 1932, and Maurice Donovan moved about 1935. But until 1935 we were the only family from 1898 until 1935. So for 40 years it remained empty.

LEONA: A lot of people were bitter about the park taking their land, but then again there's another way of looking at it. If the park hadn't taken it over, how much of it would have been owned by people from the United States? The kids wouldn't have anywhere to swim—they wouldn't be allowed access to that property. So there's two ways of looking at it.

And then along with that, it's given a lot of employment to a lot of people. Because most of the ones that lost their property to the parks were more or less guaranteed jobs, and even their children and their grandchildren still have jobs because of this takeover....

But on the other side of the coin—when the park came, a lot of the fishermen hauled their boats up on the beach, and they rotted there. It made some dependent on the parks. They lost that independence—that sort of thing that they had. (*Their fire?*) Yes—plus their incentive. "Well, I'll work on the park for 25 to 30 years. I'll retire and I'll get a park pension...."

I often think, though, if the young people could have even two months of living like we did in the Clyburn Valley—such a frugal life— still, when I look back on it, those were some of the happiest years of my life. If people could live in a wilderness where they had to fend for themselves and use their own wits to provide themselves with their food and their entertainment and everything, we'd have better people growing up. More responsible....

Homes at Cap Rouge, circa 1934

IN 1934 R. W. CAUTLEY, in his report to the federal government recommending the site of the Cape Breton Highlands National Park, wrote regarding the people who were about to be moved out:

It is difficult to understand why shore fishermen have settled in some of the places where they are found....

Many of the isolated fishing stations are in small coves or beaches below cliffs from 200 to 400 feet high. It is impossible to use schooners or anything larger than an open fishing boat, about 27 feet long, which can be pulled high up on the beach. There is no railway for the transportation of fish. During winter, the shores are beset with ice and active fishing only commences in May and is practically over by the middle of October. During the winter months, there is no means of travel except by dog sleds and snowshoes. From numerous inquiries made, I gathered that the people settle down for six months of the year to getting enough wood to keep their small houses warm, looking after a few head of stock which most of them have, and doing such odd jobs as making or mending fishing gear, making ax-handles, etc.

Usually these shore fishermen own about 100 acres of which one-fifth of an acre is in potatoes, five or six acres in rough pasture and the rest is unimproved timbered hillside. They keep one or two cows, a few remarkably fine sheep and some chickens. Most of them are extremely poor, ruggedly independent and more than usually contented. It is probable that they have been less affected by the depression of the past five years than almost any other class of Canadians.

WILFRED CREIGHTON, Halifax, handled the expropriations for the Cape Breton Highlands National Park. In an interview many years later, he said:

I minded seeing people put out of their homes. That bothered me terribly. There were cases, particularly in Cap Rouge. Most of the people were there. A woman, as a bride, had gone to that house. Had raised her family. And here's an old woman, she was being put out. And, they were as friendly and nice with me, and I reached the settlement, and I went and took the cheque and handed it over and the husband would show it to his wife and she'd burst into tears. I pleaded with the government, "Give them life tenancy." I mean, a lot of them were older people who'd only have lived five or ten years. And then the younger ones moved away, and when they started moving away.... It's one thing to be put out of your home, and another to go willingly.

Capt. Paul Chiasson— Working on Coastal Vessels

I ALWAYS HAD A LIKING FOR BOATS. When I was going to school and I used to see the gypsum boats coming in to Chéticamp Harbour, and I watched them going out. I was always—I used to make a picture—I was wondering where those boats were going, which direction would they go. I would have been curious to find out, going to England, now, which way will they go? I was always interested in boats. I don't know, there was always something in me that interested me in boats.

I left home when I was very young. I left home on a Norwegion ship called the *Dago* that was hauling gypsum from Chéticamp to Portsmouth, New Hampshire. The gypsum mine was going. I was only about 16 then. And we used to [go] to Dingwall [where they were also quarrying gypsum]—take part cargo, and come back in Chéticamp and finish our cargo, because Dingwall [harbour] never had enough water for the ship to take full cargo.

I had never travelled before. I had worked a little bit during the summer vacation. I had a little bit of money in my pocket. I was not going for the money. More or less I was going just to see what it was like to be in a big city, you know. What it was like to be at sea.

So that was my first experience at sea, on this Norwegian ship. I started as a deck boy. (*What did you do?*) Anything else that the sailors said—anything that the sailors were doing. Tying up ship, chipping, painting. But when you started those days, you had to start as a deck

boy, then ordinary seaman, then able seaman. It was my first ship....

And the pay was—I was not going, really, for money. I was going more or less to have a look around, to see the world. That's about the size of it. Because money, there was no money. The pay was nine dollars a month! I was seasick the first trip; I had never been at sea before. So, I stuck to it.

Then, that first trip that I made on the *Dago*, that Norwegian ship—when we came back—we came through the Strait of Canso, and it was a gale of wind. And there was a ship called the *Orion* that was lost, she went ashore. And the word had got in Chéticamp that it was the *Dago*. So when we came out of the Strait of Canso, we went and took shelter near Souris, P.E.I., on the lee side of the island, where we'd get smooth water. So we stayed there for 24 hours, hove through there at just dead slow speed.

First [my parents] had heard the word,

somebody had said that it was the *Dago*. Because we were due in Chéticamp. The news was not like it is today. The news had come that there had been a ship lost. (*And what happened to the Orion?*) Oh, she was a complete loss. Complete loss. I think she had a load of grain. Corn, I think....

Then, coming onto the end of the season [for] the gypsum, [the *Dago*] unloaded at Portsmouth, New Hampshire, and then we went to Baltimore to load scrap iron for Norway. There were three of us. There was myself and another fellow from Chéticamp and a fellow from Newfoundland, St. John's. And when we came back to Brooklyn, New York, there were Norwegian sailors that were waiting to be repatriated to Norway. So they said, "Well, we'll have to pay you off." So they paid the three of us off.

So I came back to Sydney. On a boat called the *Dominique*, a passenger. And there was a small coaster running from Halifax to Chéticamp which used to be an ex-rumrunner. And you could work your way back and forth. If you wanted to work, assist in working the cargo, you could get a free passage....

It was a motorboat. It was an ex-rumrunner; she was called the *Reo*.... We used to leave Halifax—today it wouldn't even be [allowed] to [carry what we carried]. You know, there were no tanker trucks like today. The gasoline used to come in 45-gallon drums. And we used to have a deckload. Because the gold mines in Gold Bar and Isaac's Harbour, they were working then. So we used to leave Halifax. As a rule, we might have had a carload of dynamite, and about 25 or 20 boxes of dynamite caps. Down in the hold. And 125 drums of gasoline on deck. No radar or nothing, in dense fog. A real time bomb!

Today, if you load dynamite, you've got to have an escort ahead of you.

In those days—all the freight along the shore used to come by these little coasters. And I'd say there were about seven or eight all running down towards Chéticamp. You could have been in a collision at any time. But at the time, I didn't know any better. The skipper was very

nervous—we used to laugh at him sometimes—but now I can see why he was nervous. I was young and I didn't realize the danger there was.

So we were very, very fortunate, very fortunate that way along the coast. Because I've seen us leaving Halifax the same thing, dense fog, you won't see anything. In those days [before radar] you had to [rely] on the compass, just a magnetic compass. If you had a deckload of [steel] drums, for example, that used to work the compass, you couldn't depend on your compass. It used to draw the compass, because of the steel. Your compass is going to be out.

I often think, how we ever made it. Not only for danger, but for the navigation of the boat. There were so many little coasters in those days, and nobody had radar in those days.

On this side of the Strait, it's not bad for fog—but from Halifax in the summer months, it's always foggy. We'd leave Halifax, and our first port of call as a rule would be Isaac's Harbour. Then we'd make our next port of call— Larry's River. There was Port Felix. We'd go in through, sometimes, White Head. Canso. We'd go to St. Peters, Arichat, West Arichat, Mulgrave, Hawkesbury, Point Tupper.

Then after we'd pass the Strait, sometimes we'd go to Havre Boucher. Then we'd go to Port Hood Island. Sometimes we had freight for the mainland—imagine that—Port Hood. And it was rough. We were unable to dock at Port Hood because it's open. There's no harbour in Port Hood. We had to drop the freight on Port Hood Island. And on our way back to Halifax, we'd stop at Port Hood Island. And we used to have a lot of freight there from Port Hood Island. They used to ship a lot of dry cod those days. There were quite a few families on the island.

So then from Port Hood Island we'd go into Mabou. Up the Mabou River. And from Mabou we'd go up to Margaree. Then Margaree, Grand Étang, and then Chéticamp. And then a lot of times we used to have dynamite for Dingwall, for the mines [the gypsum quarry].

And one time, we left Chéticamp, we stopped at Margaree to load lumber with that little boat. And it was late in the fall, beginning of December. And we never finished loading the lumber till about 10 o'clock at night, and it was dark. And Margaree is very shallow water and a bad place to get out. It was not buoyed like it is today. They just had little spar buoys. The captain said, "I don't think we'll go tonight. We'll wait tomorrow morning." Which was very stupid. I can't see it now. Because, with the experience that he had—and the glass was low from a westerly—westerly blows right into the harbour. So the next morning it was a westerly gale, so it was impossible to go out. It was blowing right into the channel.

After the storm abated, we let go the lines to go out. When we got in the middle of the channel, we hit bottom. We put the red line over the side: there was only eight feet of water, and we were drawing twelve. So there was not much chance for us to go over. We had to back off, and we tied up.

We were tied up at Margaree Harbour for two weeks, unable to get out. And here were all these little coasters going down—you could see them. And the captain pretty near went foolish, because naturally, it was his own boat and he was losing a lot of money. His freight was in Halifax.

So we had cement drums [on board]. We used to take the full ones down and the empty ones back. So while we were in Margaree, we filled all the foredeck with empty drums. And then we filled them up with salt water. To put the boat down by the heads so there'd be less draft. So we got an easterly—strong southeast or easterly wind—the current swept the channel again. It used to fill up (with sand) with westerly. (*And then the easterly wind....*) Would clear it up. So this Sunday morning it was after the easterly, we decided we'd go. And she touched [bottom] three or four times, [but] we made it right out. That was just before Christmas. Ah, geez, we laughed. The captain said, he said, "I'll never come back into this port again," he said, "even if there was 50 feet of water and no bottom!"

We arrived at Halifax I think it was about

only two or three days before Christmas. The shed was loaded with freight. We left with the two holds full of cargo. A deckload. We had a spare room for the second engineer, [but] we didn't carry a second engineer. We used to fill that up with freight, like bags of sugar. The captain's room was fairly big. He had freight. Some in the forecastle where we used to stay. We had a dory for a lifeboat—that was filled. And the top of the [wheel]house. Honest to goodness! Today you wouldn't get away with that.

(*On the top of the wheelhouse....*) Empty barrels, like mackerel barrels, and laths—we used to fill that up on top. Even sometimes he'd put cabbages in the lifeboat.

Oh, those days, boy, everything used to come by boats. You take in Chéticamp at the [gypsum] mine, they were using an awful lot of gasoline. That was all coming by boat. There was no such a thing as tanker trucks those days. Every trip, we had 100 drums of gasoline. Everything used to come by boat.

(*And was there something to go out as well?*) Not full cargoes, but there was always something. Like the empty drums. All the cod that was being dried up. We used to pick up a lot. The lobster season—we used to bring a lot of canned lobsters back to Halifax.

And one trip especially we brought some gypsum samples on that boat—[samples that were] going over to England, when the gypsum company was trying to get some contracts in England.... Like I say, not always full cargo. But there was always something....

Another thing, too, that we used to haul, every trip, we never used to fail: we always used to have between 10 and 12 puncheons of molasses. There was an awful lot of molasses used. And at the time there was an awful lot of people making that home beer, homebrew. They were making that seed beer.... And there was an awful lot of molasses being eaten, because, you know, it was the Depression, eh? The molasses used to come in puncheons. And it was good molasses, not like today. It was really thick. The same as it used to come from Barbados. Now the molasses is coming in tankers; they have tankers that carry molasses. And it's diluted then whenever it's being discharged. It's not this stuff, the real molasses.

But as far as the freight those days, like I say, there were no trucks, everything was coming by boat—everything. We were carrying flour. Sugar, molasses, gasoline, name it. Anything at all. Fertilizer, cement. Hauled all that cement for that church in Havre Boucher. Coal—we even loaded coal one time at Little Bras d'Or for Prospect on the outside of Halifax. We went to P.E.I. one time and loaded potatoes at Montague. So, we were into everything. Salt—go to Lunenburg and we used to load salt for the Robin Jones. So, you'd haul anything that was possible, wherever there was a cargo.

Because in those days all the mackerel, it was not shipped frozen or fresh like it is today. Everything was salted. Laths for making lobster traps—we used to have in the fall or early spring—well, mostly in the fall because the fishermen used to make their traps in the winter.

One time we had 10 puncheons of molasses on deck. And a puncheon was something that was hard to secure proper when it was rough. So we left Port Hood Island, it was late in the fall, it was in December again. And the boat was rolling badly. And one puncheon took off and hit the winch, and knocked the bottom of the molasses off. And when one left, they all got loose. So the captain had to put the boat head up to the wind to stop the rolling. And we had all these laths on top of the house. And I was on top passing laths to the other fellow, trying to block the barrels. And the spray

coming overboard, everything froze solid. And we had to go back to Port Hood Island, and discharge that molasses on the island, and to reload it again on the way back to take it to the mainland!

Ah, geez, those days, I'll tell you what. There was no such a thing as hours. You worked—I've seen us work—like, sailing day in Halifax, get up at six o'clock in the morning, start to load cargo at seven. Sometimes go to another pier, Pier 2, one of those big piers. Maybe take a carload of sugar or maybe a carload of fertilizer. Work all day. In the evening, say around seven or eight o'clock—they had a little boat that used to come alongside from Dartmouth, tie up alongside, where you'd put all those drums of gasoline on our deck. Now, we had to store those, eh? Rolled them, and then secured them with rope.

And then leave Halifax about 11 o'clock, midnight, after working all the time. And I had the first wheel. I'd take the wheel from midnight till four o'clock in the morning. Before getting any rest!

Capt. Paul Chiasson went on to serve on the Lady Boats as harbour defense on both coasts during the Second World War, as a tugboat captain, and as a pilot for foreign ships in Cape Breton waters. He was aboard the *Wabana* when she was cut through by the *Scythia* in 1952.

View of Chéticamp Harbour, circa 1925

Lobster Fishing with Johnny MacInnes

NOBODY WORKS HARD TODAY. It's just child's play compared to hauling them by hand. If the hauler broke on us today, we just wouldn't haul a trap—and I don't know if we could. That's about the size of it. And we wear a lot more clothes now than we did when I started fishing. I used to roll my sleeves up the day we'd start. Well, if you weren't hauling traps up you were rowing—and that wasn't the easiest thing either, especially if there was wind—and you were hot all the time. It didn't make any difference how cold it was, you'd still be too warm. So there was very little clothes that a fellow wore.

I was 13 when I started lobster fishing in 1926. That first year I fished with my father and then would go to work in the lobster factory [a cannery] after I came ashore. There were several, more than me, that worked like that. The boats then used to be ashore about seven o'clock in the morning. We'd get up about half past three. There was no Daylight Saving then—so it would be the same as half past four on this time.

We hauled the boats then at Breton Cove. We'd be at the shore and all the boats would go out about the same time. We'd put them down to the landwash. The crowd would be there and we'd shove them off. They weren't near as big as the boats now. About the biggest boat then would be about 21 feet overall. And a four-horsepower would be about the biggest. At that time there were three motorboats at Breton Cove. Several fishing with rowboats besides that. When I started off on my own, I rowed.

When I went out first I fished 110 traps, hauling them all by hand. They were heavy, but they fished them different to the way they fish them now. Then, there were 12 traps on a rope [backline] and a little kellic [a homemade anchor made of a heavy rock tied in the crotch of a branch] on each end of the rope. The rope coming up to the buoy on the surface was between the first trap and the kellic, only closer to the trap so the kellic wouldn't come up. There was just one trap taken in the boat and baited and then let out—and then you'd haul the next one. You'd run along the backline, and take one trap in and drop it out and start hauling the next one. Sometimes if there was slack enough—if you were hauling with the tide—you could haul the next trap and have it up at the edge of the boat before the other one would have to go out. If it was like that, you'd get through faster. But if you set these traps with the tide the day before, that rope would be awful hard to get up. It'd be right tight. You might have to pull the

kellic before it'd come up. If you set them with the tide I've often seen them that they'd be desperate hard to get up.

(*What does "setting with the tide" mean?*) The tide is running with the way you're setting the traps— that way the tide took them ahead as you were setting them, and they'd tighten right up. Whereas if you set against the tide, this trap would drop here and the next one would not come down with a tight rope because it would work a little closer. We have always set the traps with the tide to get them as far apart as we can. That would make them fish better.

THE MORNING OF THE FIRST DAY of the season, they go out with the boat piled high with traps, each trap already baited with fish and containing an extra rock or two to keep it down until the wood has soaked up water. After the first haul (tomorrow), when they are sure the trap will not float, this extra weight will be taken out. The traps are placed on board systematically. Each swing is made up of a long rope (the backline) with a buoy at either end. Along this backline four traps are attached with a rope bridle. When loading the boat, first a buoy is passed to a man on the boat and the rope is gathered into a pile on the deck. As each trap along that swing is come to, it is placed on board and the rope between the traps goes onto the pile. When all four traps are piled aboard together, the last portion of the backline comes on and with it the second buoy. This second buoy is tied to the first buoy of the next swing—and the process of loading up continues.

They set the traps out in long straight lines running with the shore across the fishing grounds. Johnny keeps the boat moving forward. One of the crew throws

a buoy overboard and the backline rope is dropped out behind. Then one at a time the four traps of that swing are put overboard as the rope between the traps is drawn out tight. The second buoy of that swing is untied from the first buoy of the next. That second buoy is tossed out and immediately the first buoy of the next swing is thrown overboard. They end up with a straight line of 22 buoys (one on either end of each backline) on the surface and 44 traps (four on each backline) on the bottom— the buoy ending one backline (one swing) close to the buoy where the next backline (the next swing) begins. Throughout the season they will run along these lines, gaffing the buoys, hauling and resetting the traps.

The daily routine starts out around 4:30 a.m., heading for the fishing grounds. They go first to the nets for bait. The bait for today is already in crates on the boat. "The day before's bait is what we use," Johnny told us. "We leave what we haul in the boat and we use that tomorrow. If you went out and found something tangled in the nets, there wouldn't be fish in them. So you always want to have the bait in the boat and not depend

Sometimes if there's strong tide and you set them out against the tide, they'd just go in a lump, right close together.

They shifted them just fine days. Take them all in the boat to shift them. Today we set them with the motor running slow, but those that had motors would never trust setting them with the motor running. They just took the traps in the boat and took them where they were going to set them. Then stop the motor and row them, putting the traps over one at a time.

Even then [when Johnny started], everybody here fished off their own grounds. They put the backline out first, stretched out in between the two kellics. Then they'd just take the traps out and put them on the backline [rope bridles ran from each trap to the backline], and these traps weren't shifted till they'd be taken ashore. They just stayed where they were set. This was oldest method. And whenever the lobsters would get scarce, they'd just take the traps ashore. They'd never shift them. Really, they couldn't shift them—there was too many traps

on this rope. They fished with a rowboat and I would say there would be anywhere from 30 to 40 traps on this rope. Too many traps to haul and shift. When [lobster] would get scarce they'd take every second trap off the rope so that it would help them to fish a little better. So they'd finally take them all off. [Men who fished that way] used to stop fishing before the season would be over.

That's the way I fished with my father. And the first year I fished alone—running on this backline with a kellic on each end. But after the

---

on what's in the nets. Besides, it's not much good to put bait on right fresh. It's better the next day."

A group of crates and boxes are set up in the centre of the boat. They include the measuring box (a smaller box set up on top of a crate) where each lobster goes when taken from the trap. Then there is a crate for the canners (lobsters measuring 2 3/4 inches) and a crate for the market lobsters (anything over 3 3/16 inches). These measurements *are not* for the entire length of the lobster, head to tail; rather, they indicate the length of the carapace, the solid shell covering the head and thoracic area. The size limit for markets is the same all over Cape Breton, but in some areas the size of canners allowed is 2 1/2 inches. There is a crate of today's bait (day old or better) and a box to receive old bait that is removed from the traps. Johnny: "We take the bait off [the spindle, out of the trap] every second day and put complete new stuff on. The next day we add to that. Then the next day again we take it all off. For instance, one day we put two pieces—two halves of mackerel—on. The next day we put one piece on. The next day we clean them and put two pieces

on." (*Why do you keep the old bait and not just throw it overboard?*) "The traps won't fish if you throw the bait back in the water. The lobsters just gather around that bait and won't bother going in the trap. That's the reason I do it. Some of the fishermen do throw it out. But I think the cleaner you keep the area where you're fishing, the more lobsters you'll get. We take it right into the landwash and dump it where it will wash ashore."

When fishing, Johnny runs the boat along a line of swings. The crew alternates jobs, but in these pictures Peter reaches overboard and gaffs a buoy and brings it aboard. The line is passed to Sandy and put around the hydraulic hauler, the rope coming in and gathering at his feet on deck. As soon as the first trap appears it is hauled onto the washboard by Merrill and Sandy. It is opened. Any crabs are removed. Occasionally there's a codfish or sea urchin or sculpin in the trap. The trap is shifted forward along the washboard and Johnny and Peter take out lobsters and check the bait. The lobsters go into the measuring box. By this time the second and perhaps the third trap are on the washboard. When all

four traps are up, Johnny puts the boat in gear and swings around in a tight circle, dragging the buoy still in the water. The rest of the crew finish cleaning out, baiting and closing the traps. Perhaps Peter will start measuring the lobsters, sorting canners from markets and putting the ones below legal size and any berried lobsters (those with eggs) overboard. Sandy may be putting the rubber bands on the claws of the market lobsters before putting them in their crate. By this time Johnny has come full circle and is in line with the other buoys. Merrill puts the fourth trap overboard and the line plays out. Then the third, second, and first go out. And when all the line is played out, the buoy is tossed over. And about that time the next swing's first buoy is close at hand and Peter leans out ready to gaff it and bring it on board.

When the lobsters are brought to the shore, Johnny ties his crates together and leaves them in the water among other fishermen's crates, all awaiting the arrival of the buyer. When the truck comes, the crates are hauled up, weighed and sold.

first year I cut the backline in the middle, then it was a trawl. I had a buoy on one end and a kellic on the other. I'd run on these swings of 12 traps. So you could set the traps out in one direction from the kellic today and you could set them the next day out in the other direction. And when you're through that a couple of times, you just haul the kellic in and move the whole thing and set and do the same again. And we called them "swings" because you could swing it in any direction from the kellic. That's where the name "swing" comes from. We still call them swings, but today they are not swings at all.

So then the next year again I started lobster fishing alone with a rowboat. Over the winter I made traps. And that year lobsters were only three cents a pound. Three dollars a hundredweight. That was the general price all over. They were all canned locally. But the very next year again we started shipping lobsters to Boston.

I shipped the first lobsters that I know of from the North Shore to Boston. They had shipped lobsters the year before from Big Bras d'Or. C.N.R. used to send trucks to Big Bras d'Or after them. They were going by ice cars. And we used to get good returns sometimes, and sometimes very disastrous returns. (*You wouldn't know the price beforehand?*) No, no.

I've seen getting a bill for the freight—the crate wouldn't make enough to pay the freight. This was on account of poor handling—the railroad cars weren't properly iced, I suppose. We used to ship twice a week. Well, whatever we had on this date went. We always cleaned them out twice a week. We'd go to Big Bras d'Or with one of these motorboats. There we'd have to help loading the trucks. Then come home. This was all after fishing. And we'd have to go with those lobsters regardless the kind of day it was. Have to go some pretty bad days, foggy and everything else—but we never had any disaster there.

(*Was this a co-op?*) No, fishermen were shipping individually. There were several companies buying in Boston. The first shipment that I made, the fishery officer came to the shore and he wanted to see the lobsters—I don't know why.

I think it was just to see if there was spawn in them, to dump them, to try and discourage us from shipping to Boston. (*They didn't want you to do this?*) No. Anyway, when the lobsters were put back in the crates, they took a scale to the edge of the water—it was 140 pounds that went in each crate. At that time I would have got $5.60 for those lobsters here [selling to the canning factory]. But I remember yet that I got 33 dollars clear for those lobsters I shipped to Boston. Sometimes the return was poor—but not very often.

(*I should think people that owned lobster factories weren't too happy to see you sending the lobsters away.*) No, they weren't. But after I shipped those lobsters, D.B. [MacLeod, who owned the lobster factory at Breton Cove]—he told me, "Now, I want you to come and tell me what returns you get for those lobsters." So I went to D.B. and I showed him the returns. He came to the shore and he told the fishermen to start shipping the lobsters, that he couldn't pay that kind of a price for them. There wasn't many shipped that year, but the next year again there were quite a few.

After that, we here learned how to look after the lobsters. We'd band them as soon as we'd get them out of the trap, and they weren't biting each other. We do that now. There are still some fishermen that don't look after the lobsters. I don't know, there should be a law, I would think, that you should have to look after it. If you had a bunch of hens and went out and just slammed the eggs in a basket and you didn't care if they'd break or not—that wouldn't be a very good way to make money in the poultry business. But that's the way some people handle lobsters.

The most damaging thing of all: say you have fish in a crate—like mackerel—and not clean that crate just as clean as you can—and then put lobsters in it in this dirty state—that's what kills lobsters altogether. Bacteria in that old black fish. Cleanliness is the most important thing in looking after live lobsters. Get those crates in water and clean them. There are some people that throw old bait in among the lobsters—those lobsters don't live. Today, we never put a lobster in a crate there has been bait in. We used to long ago but I found out that it was wrong.

And keep the temperature right—don't let them get too warm…. So if it's a hot day, ice is very important. When we are fishing, whenever it's warm, when we fill a crate we dump it overboard and tie it to a swing till we're ready to go in.

When I started, the lobsters weren't near as plentiful as they are now. There wasn't half the lobsters. There were several reasons for that. The spawn lobsters weren't protected at all. They were taken. There was no lobster too small, either. They were all taken. And that wasn't the killer altogether. They had been canning lobsters after the season would close, in the woods.

(*Were the traps different then?*) No, not much different. Only they've improved. They hold the lobsters better. But design was pretty much the same. There were a lot more big traps then—four-bow instead of three-bow traps. Some would be four feet long, the length of a lath. Now they're a little less than three feet. But the rope is different. We use this monoline now, and in a storm the traps go with it worse. We used to lose a lot with the manila rope too. It sank and it would chafe on the bottom, especially at the buoy. But when it was on the bottom in a storm, it would catch on the bottom and hold traps. But this monoline rope will float, it's never on the bottom—the traps go worse in a storm….

It was a gradual change. I found that we lost traps on account of kellics. I started making the traps so that they wouldn't float. Then, the manila rope used to chafe on the bottom. You only had a buoy at one end. Start hauling that and the rope would break. I figured I was losing more traps so I stopped using the kellic altogether. And now there's nobody using kellics. I made the traps so the ballast rocks stayed in. The trap may smash to pieces and still the ballast wouldn't come out. And that's the only thing that keeps them from floating away.

(*Are you aware of what's going on on the bottom?*) Over the years, yes. There was quite a while this year I wasn't aware of where we were setting, with the fog. I have landmarks ashore, and there are areas where there is hard bottom and areas where there is sand. So we try to keep the traps on hard bottom. You're fishing on this ridge for a while, and the lobsters get scarce on it—then you remember another ridge where the lobsters are picking up after a while with the traps away—so we try there. I might start at the outer edge of this ridge and then move them in the next day till we get to the inner edge of it. Then perhaps we have to skip quite a piece to get in on this other one that perhaps we have left it three or four days before. Fish there and then perhaps we'll move back to the other one again. That's the way we do it. But this summer you couldn't do much of that so far [this is early

So when I started to fish, they were really scarce. (*But they talk about years ago people getting 25 and 30,000 pounds in a season.*) Oh, that's when it started first. They were right plenty then, and they thought that they could never hurt them, never get them down any way. Finally, got caught up…. And then it was 50 cents a hundred, count [50 cents for one hundred lobsters].

But the first people who fished here were people who came from New Brunswick. Fellow came in with a factory and brought the fishermen and traps with him. They didn't fish much gear then. Then it moved on to the local people, fishing on these long strings. John Alex John X.'s father was one of the first natives to fish here, and Sandy Urquhart's father. That was quite a few years before my time. (*And were they getting big hauls?*) Yes. And no money. Before I started fishing they had been 10 cents a pound. Right after the First World War. They dropped down to three cents a pound.

Lobster Fishing with Johnny MacInnes

June 1979, three weeks into the season], couldn't see your marks on shore.

Early in the season, I fish further out. After two weeks, when these traps have soaked the water, they'll take a lot more punishment than when they're dry. The laths will break easily when they're dry. But from now on they're after soaking the water and they'll stand twice as much. If you set them inside, they roll a lot more than they do in deep water anyhow—you have to have heavier traps to fish inside, even after they soak the water. In other words, a light trap even with fine weather won't fish inside. They've got to be right still before a lobster will go in. Even if there's a little roll, if it's a light trap working around on the bottom, it won't fish.

So early in the season I keep the traps outside for the traps to soak so that they'll stand something. Now we're after moving in quite a bit. And once we move in we've got to watch the weather forecast every day. If a storm were coming tomorrow, we'd move back out again. If we're way in and we have a bad forecast we take 20 or 24 traps at a time aboard the boat. They're always safer further out. The east wind is the only thing that hurts traps here. Sometimes southeast. But northeast is good for lobsters and never smashes gear here at all.

Here, each man fishes off his own land. But I don't really think that's what helps the lobster stock. What helped the lobster stock was when we started shipping lobsters to Boston. Most of all the spawn lobsters, the berried lobsters—they're in the market size. Well, if you shipped a crate to Boston and there was a berried lobster or two—the crate was dumped. Just dumped, and you got nothing for it. There were state inspectors there. Everybody was scared of sending spawn lobsters. And they were sending shorts—ones that weren't long enough for the market—they were thrown back in the water and you got nothing for them. So that's really what helped the fishermen.

One good thing about fishing off your own. If the traps were all mixed up here, we'd lose three or four times as many as we do. The fishing is always better inside. If everything was mixed up, the fisherman that was ambitious is going to be inside where most of the lobsters are. Then you'd get a little storm and you'd lose your gear. So now...this way, each man can save the inside for later in the season.

But the big reason it was started here is that they were hauling each other's traps so much. And growling, fighting—they just had to come to some sort of mutual agreement. So the Scotchman must be just as bad as anyone else. Now, if you're seen hauling traps at someone else's place, well, you haven't any of your own traps there. So you're in trouble. (*It wasn't a conservation measure?*) No, no. (*And people still respect it?*) Oh, yes. (*And years ago, if they came out and found someone else's traps on their grounds?*) Oh, they used to cut the traps, destroy them. Sometimes they'd haul them up and set them back on the grounds they belonged to. That's still done. And years ago, they'd cut the traps away if somebody set on another man's territory. I think it's a good rule. And the reason it was started was to avoid this wrangling and haul-

ing each other's traps and growling about it, one fellow accusing the other.

They used to have a superstition here, if you wore grey mitts—I never paid any attention to it—but they said something would happen to you before the season would be over—disaster of some nature. And they didn't like to see a woman coming to the shore. That's when I started fishing first. And white mitts were worn. But there isn't a word about that today.

(*And was there a superstition about sod?*) Not a superstition. Some people can't urinate in a boat [over the side]. But if they took a piece of sod and stood on it—they could. (*I thought the piece of sod would protect you if you found a body at sea.*) Oh, that was supposed to be terrible hard luck. I never heard anything about the sod, but it was supposed to be bad luck to find a body at sea. And there were stories of things that happened to people that found a body—they were dead themselves before the year was over. I suppose they died through nervousness. They were supposed to die anyway. I know I used to hear my mother talk about that. She was from New Campbellton—there was somebody over there found a body and he died before the year was out. It was awful hard luck anyway.

Different times fishing, I'd see something. I'd certainly take the body, if it was one, but I'm telling you I was scared it was going to be one. Lots of things that looked an awful lot like a body—but when you'd come to it, it was something else.

On June 17, 1973, the worst storm in living memory struck Cape Breton Island—winds up to 71 miles an hour bringing enough snow to strand cars on Smokey and Kelly's Mountains. The photo at the top of the page is of Johnny MacInnes, taken when they were setting traps the first day of that season (May 15th). The photograph above was taken the morning after the storm. The boat was anchored at the breakwater (completely underwater in the picture) and her stern anchor let go, bringing her broadside to the breakwater and filling her. Lloyd MacInnes, Kenny Matheson and Ian MacDermid went out in a dory to tie onto her and pull her to the wharf.

Theodore Rideout— "I Went Sealing"

THERE WERE 9 OF US from Neil's Harbour. The rest were from Newfoundland, all parts of Newfoundland.

We had to walk to North Sydney. Took us eight hours to go to Ingonish the first day. With a pack on our back, 25 or 30 pound. Next day we walked up D. B. MacLeod's North Shore. We walked in the sleigh track. I'll always remember, when we got up to D. B. MacLeod's our feet were wet, and an old woman gave us dry socks to put on. And the next day we got our feet wet walking across Englishtown. Across the ice.

That day we ended up in Bras d'Or. And the next day went to North Sydney. Took us four days. We stayed while an old ship came from Halifax. We met her in Louisbourg. Another day or two, the Newfoundlanders came aboard. Came over and came aboard. We started out the 4th of March. And we went to the ice.

I'll always remember it. We got up 10 or 15 miles north by St. Paul's, we struck the ice. That night—it was a moonlight fine night. The first ice we struck, she started to go like this. Rocking. And we were at seals that night. So he stopped and he stayed there all night. And next morning we got 90.

Come on a storm from the southeast, thick-a-snow. And old Capt. Marley from Trinity Bay, Newfoundland, was the captain of the ship. He blew the whistle and all hands went on board. He started up the Gulf. Went for four days and four nights—the vessel—through the ice. We went up, I guess up around Anticosti, the other side of—you couldn't see any land, anyway. And we got stuck. And there we lay in one spot for six weeks and three days. Couldn't move. If you'd get out and look at the ship, look back at it, there was no sign of her, it was like a snowbank.

But we never got any seals, and we stuck in the ice too long. And we had nothing to eat. Lots of food aboard. All we had to eat was hardtack and molasses. She had lots of grub aboard. She had everything. For the sailors, captain, and doctors—they had all kinds of fresh meat, ham and eggs, and porridge and bacon. Sealers never got any of that. There were 175 sealers. And 25 of a crew. The crew didn't go sealing. They stayed on the ship all the time. They got all kinds of grub. We got nothing. That's what we got—old hardtack and old fish with the skin and all on it.

I don't know how to tell you this. There's a long story. I'd be four days trying to tell you.

We got no seals. But I used to go out on the ice with some old fellows from St. John's, Newfoundland. And we left one morning at seven o'clock. And we walked till seven that night. All day on that ice. We got one seal. They were just out looking, see if they could find any. They came back with one seal. Well, you'd sooner do that than lay around the ship all day.

We did nothing while we were jammed in the ice, only roaming around the ship, go out and try to kill a few sea-birds and pick them and eat them. Bake them. Edgar Lillington of Neil's Harbour used to bake some buns for us. We never got any bread, only hardtack—so he used to bake buns. Molasses buns. So we used to enjoy them. It's that bad of a story, I don't know if I should be telling it to you.

Well, it's starvation. We had starvation on the ship. And all kinds of meat aboard of her. Twenty-five quarters of meat going spoiling—big western quarters of meat—we didn't get any. Not a crumb. Only the captain was getting that, and officers and doctors. They got all kinds of steaks. We got a roast beef Sunday—a bone. And through the week we got a pot of pea soup. And for breakfast in the morning, there's a big barrel of hardtack in the corner there, and a bucket of molasses over there. And you go and take a hardtack out of the barrel. If you had good teeth, and had some molasses, and put it in your cup. And tea—they used to call that "switchel"—because that was boiled over and over and over and over. And that was our breakfast, every morning.

Well, come dinnertime we'd have potatoes with hake, old hake—I don't know if you know what hake is—skin and all on, just like they come out of the water. You eat that, if you had a good stomach. They would boil it up. We had different cooks from what the officers had. We had three old cooks that had never cooked be-

fore. Well, they had real chefs, the captains and officers and doctors. There were two doctors on it. When they'd pass through in the morning, you could smell the bacon and eggs. We never got one bit.

And come a mild day, and we had to get up on deck. About 25 quarters of western beef was getting mouldy; we had to wash the slime off of it. Fresh water with baking soda in it. To wash the slime off the meat—it was spoiling. (*So you knew the meat was there.*) We knew the meat was there. What we should have done was raided the ship! You couldn't believe it unless you saw it!

If we'd have got some seals, I guess we'd have got some good grub. If we didn't get any seals, we got no grub. And we had no tobacco. But the Newfoundlanders that were out the year before had their tobacco. They knew what was going to happen. If we didn't get seals, we wouldn't get any tobacco. And no grub, either.

I was thinking about it in bed the other night—up there, stuck in the ice. And I was telling my wife yesterday—that's where you used to see the rough days out there on the ice fields. The winds were blowing nor'west. You couldn't see anything. There was no woods, there was no nothing—only ice and snow and wind.

Then we got lousy—I'm telling you everything! We all got lousy. And that wasn't too good. You get out on the ice and try to pick your shirt. This is a beautiful story to go in a magazine, I guess! I guess it's going to go, but I don't give a damn. This is right. It's all true, what I'm telling you.

And our old cooks used to cook puddings. And you couldn't eat it—there was no way you could eat it. And when we got out of the ice, you'd look back and there was a big pile of puddings, big as this house! About 5000 gulls trying to eat it. It was made out of hardtack! I guess they couldn't do that today with a bunch of people, eh?

I was only young, right young. I was the youngest one aboard perhaps. Fifteen, I suppose I was. Perhaps 16. (*Where did you sleep?*) Well, they had bunks, all around the wall, like that. About three high, three or four in a bunk—there were four in ours—right around like that. It was on the deck. But down, right there [below us], she was full of coal down there. And when the bunkers got empty, we had to hoist that coal out of there. So you know what kind of a mess there was—there was ice and coal everywhere we slept.

We had to hoist it back, carry it back to the bunker in wheelbarrows. (*Through the place where you slept?*) Through the place where we slept. (*And the place you slept, was it cold or warm?*) Fair. (*Fair. Nothing was good.*) No, there was nothing good about it. (*And where did you eat then?*) Eat right there. And no table, we never had a table. Just stood up wherever you could, and eat. Just sitting up like I and you, and eat away.

So, after the six weeks was up, there was another big storm come. And a swell got under the ice, and opened it up, opened it up. And we got back. When we got to St. Paul's, we came out of the ice. He landed us in North Sydney. There was nothing running then, no roads. You had to walk it. Or run it! We got down by an old boat from Ingonish. An old fellow was up after

freight. He brought us back here, landed us in Neil's Harbour, Jimmy Brewer from Ingonish.

So we landed. We made two dollars and 40 cents each. We ended up with a dollar and eight cents. Anybody had oilclothes, and stuff like that—they took that off of him. (*From the $2.40?*) Yeah, that's right. Well, they'd pay for a few suits of oilclothes, out of everybody. A dollar and eight cents, that's what we got, when we were cleared up. Well, 240 seals among that many men. And the spring before, she got 12,000. They made $400 apiece, the spring before that.

(*Did you ever go back again?*) No, I never went back again. But I would have. 'Cause I know that times changed after that. I'd have gone back next year, yeah. (*Why didn't you go?*) Well, I never got a chance to go. That old boat was seized in New York, with a load of rum.

It was a good experience in a way. We never had any tobacco, and we never had any grub. And I'm telling you. The holes in hardtack? Some of them had maggots in them. (*Couldn't have been worse.*) No, couldn't have been any worse. We all gained weight! All the young fellows gained a lot of weight—it must have been the fresh air out in the Gulf of St. Lawrence! It wasn't grub, eh?

Hattie Carmichael,
St. Ann's

The Harvest Train Song

STEVE WHITTY, *Ingonish Beach*: Mike MacDougall's father [Dan Rory], he was the awfullest man ever to make up a song about you. He made one there about where we went to the Harvest in 1920.

People had been going for years and years before that. That was the first year I went. I was 23. In my prime of life. At that time you'd go over to North Sydney on the first *Aspy* and buy your train ticket—28 dollars and a quarter from North Sydney to Winnipeg—one way.

Before we left Ingonish, you'd be hearing the talk of it. Oh, they'd be there and meeting you, to get you to go to work for them. [Steve sings:]

> "It being on the fourth of August
> 　　we left our friends so dear
> On board the steamboat *Aspy*
> 　　for Sydney we did steer
> It being on the evening of the fifth
> 　　our tickets we produced
> 　To take us all to Winnipeg,
> 　　that place that we all cursed."

Because when we got there we couldn't get a job. And we were shy on money. You had to get grub enough in North Sydney, and you know what that was like after a few days in an old suitcase. It was that hard it was like bullets. My dear soul.

There were jobs in Winnipeg. But we went too early. It wasn't our fault. That was the time that was advertised in the papers. There was no place for food along the way, really, you couldn't get anything. You'd get the train stopping here and there, at a little store—get a bottle of pop or something like that. We were dying for that. The water was awful on the train. "We travelled for six days and nights, our provision it got slim/ And to get off the iron horse we sure were in bad trim/ Both sleepy, dirty and hungry we scarcely could crawl/ And to be without cold water, we found the worst of all."

There were 820 on our train. And there was 800 on a train three-quarters of an hour after. But when we got to Winnipeg there was nothing to do. All seven of us could have got on, but they only offered us the smallest kind of wages. Because harvesting hadn't started and they thought they had us right there. Some fellows on the street told us the Harvest had got started in Moose Jaw, Saskatchewan. That was 400 miles from Winnipeg. But still and all, you could go that 400 miles for two dollars—half a cent a mile was the rate. We went to Moose Jaw.

"Oh Jim, he was quite nervous, as any you ever saw/ He bid goodbye to Tom and Frank when we landed in Moose Jaw/ 'May the Lord above look down,' he said, 'have mercy unto me/

The Harvest Train Song

For here we are both one and all, no work that I can see.'" When we got there it was the same damn thing. Harvesting hadn't started. So there we were, the seven of us on the street. "Now Jack he was quite surly, and unto us did say/ 'Oh pity my condition and warning take by me/ If my father had done justice when first out west I roamed/ And taken down the shotgun and broke some of my bones.'"

By and by we saw a fellow coming toward us. Asked us were we looking for work. Told him yes. "We walked along on Main Street all looking for a job/ We met a man who said to us, 'Go get on a waterworks/ I'll pay you five dollars a day, charge forty cents for meals/ You will not go a-harvesting if you'll accept this deal.'" That didn't leave us a hell of a lot, but we were satisfied to go. But it was a bad place to work. "We went to work next morning in that God-forsaken place/ Nothing but French Canadians, and the flies, they'd eat your face/ Down in the hole went Frank and Jack, in mud and mar they strayed/ Which caused them to look around, say, 'A damn short time we'll stay.'"

Every evening we'd go out to see if we could find out anything about the harvesting. "It was in that place of poverty we lasted for five days/ There was no place else to eat or sleep, not even to wash your face/ It was then we took the notion, another job to hunt/ We went to seek and we did meet the man they call Beaumont."

The boss we hired with in the Harvest said he would give us six dollars a day and free board and free bed. We had a great place there. Didn't work hard at all. The work was stoking the grain. It was all cut by machinery. It would go on this rake and it all went in sheaves and it was tied and thrown out. And you came along and stoked them together. Leave them standing in the field to ripen. We only had two jobs, stoking and thrashing. After the grain was all ripened on the stalks, we had two horses each to haul it in to where they were thrashing it. Wonderful experience. I never forgot it nor I ever will, because I loved it.

But I went to the Harvest just the once. For us, that was the end of the Harvest Train. It was awful going out there. I enjoyed it because there was a bunch of us good fellows together. But there was some of them harvesters awful, for stealing and breaking in stores and things like that. The people were frightened to death. I don't see why they didn't shoot them. They fired out everything. All sorts of clothes. Boxes of shoes and everything else. And you know those small buckets of jam—well, boy, anybody on the train wanted jam could get it with no trouble. Carry loads of that a-board the train.

Train would start in North Sydney. There were 22 cars. And it was breaking in and stealing from the time we left. Because

Harvesters at the CPR station, Winnipeg, circa 1900

Dan Rory MacDougall, piper

some that were on the train were used to this, were at it before. They'd tell the conductors where they wanted to stop, and the poor fellows would have to stop. God only knows what they wouldn't do. I'm not telling you a lie. I've seen them going out and bringing aboard the train God only knows how many hens they took out of a henhouse. And when the train was going as fast as ever she could go—fastest I ever saw was 48 miles an hour—because the mileage was on posts and that's all you had to do—everyone had a watch, seeing how many miles we were going an hour. Anyway, bring those poor hens in and

they wouldn't kill them—they'd let them go. Fire them out through the windows. One by one you'd see the hens go. The poor things. These were mostly young fellows.

(*You're not saying everyone did this.*) No, no, no. Just two, say, in the car I was in. And they would get together wherever the train would stop. But after we crossed Québec Bridge, the soldiers were there lined up with their guns. "Now you touch one of these stores and we'll touch you." There was no more stealing after we crossed Québec Bridge. They had soldiers right along, wherever they slowed down for coal and water and things like that—the soldiers would be there. And it's a good thing the stealing stopped because the cars were already piled up with things they never used. Neckties, shirts, shoes—boxes of little kids' shoes—shoes with copper toes. See they were no good, fire them away.

(*What did you do that was bad?*) Well, I suppose I did my share. But I didn't do any stealing, I can tell you that. I never took anything. I had a dread over me. I was 23 and there were lots there only 17 and they didn't know what badness meant. You could talk to people and tell them it wasn't right to be bringing hens and stuff like that in the train—which we did. They'd just laugh at you.

(*If this was the case, I'm surprised they kept those harvest trains running.*) Stopped after that year. She never took anyone, only students going to college after that. They weren't allowing anyone to go who was on the train before. And then they started getting

Cape Bretoners "on the harvest" at Rathwell, Manitoba, 1914

The Harvest Train Song

better gear on the fields and now I don't think even the college boys are going.

(And you could say it was a wonderful experience. How could it be so good? You went out too early, food was all ruined, had to work on the waterworks, and then you were just lucky to get some harvest work....) Yeah, it was all luck. *(And that was the best job you ever had?)* Well, it was the best job I ever had with a boss onto it. He was just like a father to us all. Told us he'd give us six dollars a day and free board—and when he paid us off, he paid us off with seven. Straight time. So he was a good guy. Seven dollars a day in 1920 was big money. I went there in August—I think the 12th of August we hired on—and my brother-in-law, Mike's father—he and I came home the last of October. A little over two months. And I had something clear over 400 dollars. Went with nothing but my fare. And Dan R. MacDougall put at the end of the song: "So now my song is over, no more I have to say/ But we will soon be going back to that place we call South Bay/ Our boats and trawls we'll now fit, for the eastern piece prepare/ To get us some provision and some clothing for to wear."

Dan R. would come in here now, sit around sizing up you and I. That's what he'd done going to the Harvest. Had 22 verses in that song, going to the Harvest. And I never knew he was doing it. When we were still there, he just worked it for me. He didn't have it finished. "There's none left but Dan and Steve, the Harvest for to win/ We would not disappoint the man or leave him in bad trim."

Oh, songs were our entertainment. Indeed they were. And there was a great deal of singing in that home. Oh, my dear man. And you know, people don't do this anymore. There's not the gimp enough in them anymore. What I call gimp, well, you've got to be full of life.

John A. Wilkie, Sugarloaf, and Effie Fitzgerald, Aspy Bay

Eddie and Simon Fraser

EDDIE FRASER, *Bay St. Lawrence*: We walked, me and Simon, we walked all over the Cabot Trail when there was no road, only to go by foot or snowshoes in the wintertime, and on horseback. Couldn't get there with a car.

SIMON FRASER: Just a little path.

EDDIE: Just a little path from there to Chéticamp. Snowshoe run from Pleasant Bay way into Chéticamp.

We were born at Pollett's Cove but we had moved up to Pleasant Bay. My father was the last family to move out of Pollett's Cove. Used to walk over the Big Barrens. Walked to the North Shore. We walked everywhere. Didn't think nothing of it at the time, nothing.

SIMON: There's a MacKinnon—he's living today—he left Black Point and started walking up to Pleasant Bay. Walked over the mountain okay—got along good over the mountain. When he got as far as Pollett's Cove, he went out on the drift ice there—and started up on the drift ice toward Pleasant Bay. Boy, he got about halfway up, the wind came southeast off the land, started to blow the ice out. So he had to climb the bank there—halfway up, I guess—and there was just a rock out in the side of the bank, like a shelf, he called it, big enough just for him to lay there anyway.

He lay there all night long. And that was in February. And it was a real cold night that night too, I remember. He came to our house the next morning. And I know it was 10 below or more. And he said when he came to the house—aw, he was shivering like a leaf—he said when he tried to get up after staying there all night, in the morning—no way. He couldn't get up with the coat on. He had to open the coat off—pull one sleeve out and then the other—then get ahold of the coat. And he had a hard time pulling it out of the ice where it froze.

EDDIE: You know what happened to me one time? I was over the Cabot Trail—over Cape North way—there was no road there or anything, just the trees were blazed. And it got dark on me, I couldn't see the blaze in the trees. I stayed there all night. There was some snow on the ground and I finally made a place there. I had no matches or anything. I had no lunch. I stayed out all night and before I'd freeze, I had to jump up and walk around all night. God almighty, I'd jump around, keep myself warm, before I'd freeze to death.

I was all right—but for three days I was feeling cold in my bones. And one fellow told me, "You're liable to get a cold out of that, Eddie." I said, "I don't think so." I didn't get a cold out of it.

(*You were out there in the dark. Did you see anything?*) Nothing. Oh...you mean ghosts or something. No, I never saw a ghost. But I have seen a forerunner of a living person.

I was living at Ingonish. Used to play cards at a place. And Janet MacKay was her name, she used to come up there playing cards. And I was sitting in the kitchen, waiting for them to come up. You know, three or four of us—everybody used to play cards. And I was in the kitchen and I saw her coming in the door. And she started laughing, smiled, laughing. I didn't think anything of it. I thought she'd stay in the kitchen, but she went into the living room. So I went in, asked Murdoch Dan—"Did Janet MacKay come in here?" He said, "No." And I had seen her coming in the door, smiling, laughed at me. That was a forerunner.

I told her about it later. She told me, that's nothing. And nothing ever came of it. Nothing.

(*Was it a forerunner of something that was going to happen?*) Well, the only thing I ever heard of that was, if you see the forerunner of a living person—if he's coming towards you, he'd have a long life. If he was going away from you, he wasn't going to live a long life. If they were going away, they were going to die soon. (*Did they ever frighten you?*) No, never scared me.

SIMON: I've actually seen—well, I've heard it. This is a true story. We were living in Pleasant Bay, way down at what they'd call the Lower End at that time. And there was a bunch of us came to our house that night, to play cards.

EDDIE: It was on a Sunday, wasn't it?

SIMON: Well, it was on a Sunday night, yes. And oh, it must have been about 12 o'clock when they all left. So we got ready and we all went to bed. And after we went to bed—well, we had been playing in the kitchen. We had taken the chairs away from the table after we were through. And after we went to bed we heard the chairs, someone dragging them over to the table, and they started dealing the cards, fancy dealing.

EDDIE: I remember that…. We all got up, every one of us.

SIMON: This was going on for a while. Something's going on there, someone's playing cards.

We got up and looked around.

The chairs were the same way, the cards were the same way as we left them. Couldn't see anyone near them, not a thing.

(*Did you talk to one another about this?*) Oh yes. Same time. Everybody in the house heard it. That's how I know it was right. One fellow might have heard it, well you'd say, might imagine—but everybody heard it and everybody got up. And everything was the same way as we left them.

So I took the cards and I threw them in the stove. And we all went back to bed. And nothing happened. (*Did you ever play again?*) Not that way, not the kind of games we were playing. (*What kind of game?*) Well, it was this dirty talk and girls and boys, and how anyone could have such a mate, do such a thing.

EDDIE: It wasn't gambling at all. But it wasn't proper. (*And do you think that was why you were hearing things?*) **SIMON**: Well, I don't know. I couldn't see any other reason. Some people say you're not supposed to play cards on Sunday…. (*After that, did you change?*) Oh yes. I don't think I ever played that game since. And I never heard the cards since.

EDDIE: But this isn't a story that was made up at all. I was there too.

I was going down to a dance one night. And after I crossed the gate, you know, I went down a little ways, and I was walking along and I felt something like that, you know, a little pull on my coat. I took a look around, did I catch a tree? There were no bushes there, my coat never got hooked in a bush, I know that. So I kept going again, and it grabbed my coat again.

That's the truth. Got my coat again and gave it a good pull, and he pulled me back a couple of steps.

I could feel like a chill going through me, and I got right light, and the hairs all standing up on my head. I said, "I'm not going to run—he's going to catch me anyway."

I never saw anything after that. But he pulled me back a couple of steps—now what was that?

Salmon Fishing on the Margaree River

JOHNNY (STEVEN) WHITE: There's no salmon in this world equal to the Atlantic Salmon, as far as flavour is concerned. And I have fished with people that fished all over the world, and I guess they've eaten and tasted every salmon that was on the face of the earth—this is number one. And this is number one for them to catch. Another thing, this Margaree River was number one to fish regardless if there was salmon or not, the pleasure of being on it. Because it was clear of flies, clear of mosquitoes with the exception of maybe a muggy day there may be a few—but that only lasts for a very short time—and the short walk you have from where you leave your car to every pool.

And even one poor fellow from New Jersey made three trips here one summer. And his third trip—I knew him well for years here—he had a heart condition and I don't see yet how his doctor allowed him to make those trips and fish—and he hooked a salmon down here at the Forks Pool and he died in the water with the fish on.

(*I guess there are salmon fishermen who'd want to die that way.*) Well, that's it. That's it.

And he once told some of his own countrymen—and I was right alongside of him—it was a beautiful glorious day and the sun shining and everything, and they were talking about the fishing wasn't any too good right at the time, but he said, "Look, my dear friend, fish or not, this is the place for me. Just look around and see those mountains. Fish or no fish, this is it for me."

The day he died, there just happened to be two fellows on the opposite side of the river, when they saw this happen. And I think they had chest waders on. And they went right through the river, went right over—and he was only up to his knees in the water. But that didn't make any difference, see, it was the heart. These two fellows went right over and one fellow took the rod and the other fellow got ahold of him and pulled him ashore, laid him down and took off on the run for the doctor. Doctor came down; the man was dead.

But the other fellow saved the fish. Now that's how much that that man loved the Margaree River....

And there was an old Dr. Park, from Baltimore, the John Hopkins'. He'd be coming here for years and years and years—and I got to know him. He was 91 and he wanted to die and be buried here. And he's buried over the river at the Wilson United Church. Now that's how much he thought of the Margaree River. And his wife buried in Baltimore—can you imagine?

(*When fishermen came down, how long would you be with someone, as a guide?*) Well, they'd generally stay for the full week, you know, six days. Some of them might be more. And some might be as low as one day. Some would make reservations ahead and have a guide for them, through the hotels. (*And what would be your responsibility, what would you do?*) Well, of course, some of them come and they've never fished before. You've got to give them casting lessons. And then there's another thing you can't do—you can do it but it's certainly not right—to take a man or woman that never cast into a pool where there's a few salmon and some expert fishermen—you're going to jumble up everything. Because if you disturb a salmon at all, he's gone, he's not going to look at a fly. If you nip a salmon with a hook, he's not going to touch that fly till maybe the next day. Because the lighter that you can drop your fly on the water, the better the chance you have of that salmon coming after it. There's the difference in fishing.

So I'd have to take my man to a pool where I was pretty sure there were no fish. And if there were no fish there were no fishermen. You take them there and maybe spend a half a day—and I've seen it happen, just a half a day and then they could get out a line and the current then would take it. Once you get the line out in front of you—the fly would go down, and if there was a salmon down around where that fly was reaching, and if he was in the mood of taking it, he'd take it whether it was an expert fisherman or not. I've had that luck in my career of guiding—take them out and just give them the half a day casting lessons, and in the afternoon I took them to a pool where I *knew* there were a couple fish, and I've seen it happen that they caught them.

(*So you don't try to drop the fly right on the fish?*) Oh, no. You fish on an angle. The fly has got to be moving with the current. You don't drop it directly over the salmon at all. Drop it a piece above him and the current takes it and he sees it moving. Then there's the other thing again: maybe this fly gets down right where that salmon is, the salmon will raise. He's not too anxious for it. He'll raise and you'll see the wave, and when you see that little wave, well now, he's not too fussy about taking it. You pull that away, just as quick as you can, coil up your line. Keep that same amount—don't put any on the reel— and wait for about two minutes. And then that

salmon goes back again to his resting place. Don't cast right immediately because he's not there. But he's got his resting place.

All right. You just wait about two minutes. Then you cast again about the same way as you did before. And if he wants that fly he won't miss it the next time. He'll take it. Then, all right, when you got the salmon on, what are you going to do? You've got to watch these new beginners. You're supposed to put your rod right up to the sky. Let the rod and the reel do the work. The way I always fished, if I figured it was a 10-pound salmon, I'd have that salmon in in 10 minutes. A pound to the minute. But a lot of these beginners—and some of the old ones—they like to keep the salmon on for possibly a half an hour. They get a thrill out of playing him. But the longer you got your salmon on, the bigger the chance you have of losing him. I was told that right from old-time fishermen—and good fishermen. They told me the first five minutes that your fish is hooked—and he's never hooked better after that. Every move and every jump that he makes, that hole is wearing out—and then if he gets one fraction of slack, the hook is out and he's gone. Put everything that's in your gear into that fish the first five minutes; don't wait till you have him on twenty minutes before you start putting power to him.

And you can't just haul him out. You'll break your gear to pieces. Look, this is what you have to have your fly tied on—that's on six-pound test. But the flexible rod and your reel, that's what's doing the work. A person would almost tell you that you were a liar, that you could never bring a 20-pound fish in with the like of that. But that's the way it's done. The rod is flexible, and every little jerk, the rod bends. And then there's the tension on your reel, the drag on your reel—I always put about a pound and a half pressure on the fish. I learned that from the old-timers. Just hold it steady at about a pound and a half. Then that fish will jump that high out of the water—four feet I've seen them. Well, when he jumps like that, that causes slack and you've got to keep your rod up in the air. Because if you lower your rod down, he'll come out of that water and get his tail over that leader and it's broke. But if you keep the rod up, when he comes down, that jerk, the rod bends with it.

(*When do you give him the line?*) Well, he'll take it. Whenever you feel that he's going out. Of course, there you go again—you've got to have no less than 100 yards of backing besides your mainline. A 30-foot line and 100 yards of backing and a 9-foot leader. And the leader—I have them tapered from 15-pound down to 4—15, 12, 10, 8, maybe 6 and 4. I splice the leader together. Four-pound

Phillip Hannigan and his son Jimmy, after a day's guiding, with the Buck family

test—that's pretty weak. But I have caught salmon with four-pound test on the 12-foot maple rod—and a homemade maple rod, that's pretty stiff. You've got to be mighty careful. No pressure. Very little. Because that rod is almost as stiff as that broom. Wouldn't do for a greenhorn to be trying to do that, you know. And as I said before, the longer you have him on, the greater your chance of losing him—and with a four-pound test and that stiff rod, you'd have to be mighty careful.

(*Ever catch a salmon and he just comes in?*) Aw, no. He'd have to be sick before he'd do that. No, it's go from you instead of come to you. And whenever they start to go, let them go. Let him run out because if you try to stop him he'll break your leader. They tire themselves. And when they start to get very tired, they start to come up to the surface; you'll see their fin come over the water. But they're still dangerous as long as they're on their belly. But if you see them getting over on their side, they're getting pretty slack. That's when you're landing a salmon at a beach, you'd just bring him in gradually. But when he's coming on his belly be very careful—he can still turn around and get away from you in a hurry. But if they happen to flop over on

their side, he's pretty slack then. And the other thing, there's such a thing as dead water, there's no oxygen in that—you get a fish over in the dead water, he'll collapse a lot quicker than in the current. Even doctors told me that. If there's such a thing as dead water at all around that pool, get him in there. The current is where the oxygen is.

All the pointers that I got in fishing—it's a peculiar thing—it's from two Duncans. Mind you: a Duncan MacDonald and a Duncan MacKenzie. They told me all about the fish and what to do. And that Duncan MacKenzie, up the Northeast there, he was an old Scotchman, of course. And witty. People used to get an awful kick out of him at the river. The answers he'd give.

Duncan MacKenzie. Good fisherman. He knew his business. It was from him and Duncan MacDonald that I learned. I started out with trout first. But like MacKenzie told a fellow who caught his first salmon—"You're ruined for the rest of your life now." There's an awful terrific thrill to catching salmon, you know.

Now Duncan MacDonald, he taught me a lot of things. He taught me, when your salmon is downriver with 75 yards of your line out, he's boss, he's got command. It's only luck any more if you ever get him back up again. Which is right. You've got to take him against the current. You can't put any pressure in God's world on a fish then, if he's that far away. So you've got to watch for that. You can chase them sometimes, because sometimes they take off from one pool to another—downriver. If they started upriver it's all the better, because you'll kill them a lot quicker. They'd have the current to fight along with the pressure on your reel. When they take off down, rather than have them strip all your line down to the backing and then break your leader—and that has happened—you've got to take off on the run as fast as you can go and get ahead of him, if you can. Run along the bank—if you can get along. And sometimes you have to go out in the water to get by certain places—bushes and limbs. Oh, it's the old story, just like music. You could learn something every, every, every day, regarding fishing. I'll be 77 in September, and I guided 41 years exactly.

The guide could hook the fish—and a lot of them would have you do it—then give them the rod and let them play it. A lot of them wanted that. The way I look at it, the main thrill is in hooking the fish—then after that, it's a worry. They wanted the worry....

(*Over 41 years of watching that river. When you started were there a lot of salmon in the river?*) Oh, for God's sake, don't be talking. This is where the change comes in. It didn't make any difference what day you'd go up to the river that time, you'd see fish—but you're not going to catch a salmon every time that you'd see him. It's just when he's in the mood to take. But that was the days of the fishing. Aw, man, you'd always see them. But today, you're lucky if you can see a fish, if you can see one of them. This was one of the best rivers in the world one time, the Margaree River here.

So little by little, I learned. I was 15 years old when I got the first salmon. And around the river here—I'm not blowing, there's no question about it—I caught one hell of a whack of salmon on this Margaree River.

Margaree River in Flood

JIMMY HANNIGAN, *guide*: If the water was anyways good shape at all, more fish would come in. (*What do you mean by good shape?*) Well, I mean if the water was up a good high. Say right now the water is terrible low. Awful low. And it gets warm and the fish don't like it as well. But when there's a freshet, a big rain, it cleans the river out and it makes clean water—good cold water for the fish—and they'll come right in.

And I'll tell you another thing that's hurting our rivers today—at least in my opinion of it—is lumber woods. (*How do you mean?*) Well, it won't hold the snow. Where they cut all those woods off miles of it around, the snow in the spring melts as fast as it can.

I remember in St. Ann's—I worked in there with twelve feet of snow. (*In among the trees?*) Yes. Well, you see, that'd take it probably two months to melt. Which kept the river up high. But now it'll wash right out once you get hot weather. There's nothing to hold that snow.

And the same with the rain when it's raining: the shade of those trees cooled the ground and it wouldn't go down in the ground so much—it would run off to the river when the ground was wet enough. But today it's got nothing—it's just like a prairie—just dry land now.

We used to get big freshets one time. We don't get them any more. We don't get the water. This here farm was all washed out one time with a freshet when we had a sawmill here. Over there—that was the mill dam out that flat there. And this high water came and the dam broke out, and we lost a lot of lumber, and it undermined the barn that was down there, too. The only thing that held the barn was the piers on

the centre of the barn—they held—and it was rocking like that.

There was a cow and a yearling and the horse in the barn. And the flooring that the cow was on wasn't spiked—and they floated from under her. And she broke the rope she was tied to and swam out underneath the sill of the barn. We had a pile of slabs out there—it was about fifteen feet high—and that was the only thing she could see clear of the mountain. And she made for that. And she got up on that. Well, she couldn't get off it, and she was stranded on the slab pile.

And we got a rope on the yearling—oh, the water—there was about ten feet of water out along there—it started undermining the house at that corner, dug a hole over eight feet deep. It was lucky it didn't hurt the house any, kept working out. And we got the yearling and pulled him through the water and got him in the house here. When the water was high, we thought the house was going to go. My father took my mother and the three of us and got us on the side of the bank and down to my grandfather's—he lived down below.

And he came back here, and the next morning there were three or four fellows from up the road came down with ropes. My father got the ropes on himself, and went out and got them on the cow, and they pulled the cow off the slab pile and over through the water to the house.

And the road down below here at the end of this field—that whole side of that mountain came down, shut the road off, shut the brook off and everything—they had to build a road across over the top of the mountain to get out of here in the winter.

(*And that's because of how much water came down the Margaree River at one time?*) Yeah. (*And today?*) You never see it coming up over the banks hardly. Very seldom. No, it was an awful freshet. (*But it made for a better salmon river?*) Yes. Yes.

Duncan MacKenzie

This fellow was talking about a big fish he caught—oh, I guess it was supposed to be a tremendous fish. My father said, "Well, I was out fishing one time and I caught a salmon, and when I took him ashore—he had a lantern in his mouth." And he said, "You know, the lantern was lit." And the fellow, more in fun than anything else, he said, "You know, I don't believe that. That's impossible." "Well," my father says, "you take 20 pounds off your fish, and I'll blow out the lantern."
—Kenneth MacKenzie, about his father Duncan

Josie Matheson Bredbury

I HAVE A LITTLE GAELIC PRAYER my mother always taught us, from the 23rd Psalm:

"Is e Dia féin a's buachaill dhomh, cha bhi mi ann an dith. Bheir e fainear gu'n luidhinn sios air cluainibh glas' le sìth. Is Fòs ri taobh nan aimhnichean théid seachad sios gu mall. A ta e ga mo threòrachadh, gu mìn réidh anns gach ball."

Mama taught us that. And there was another one that she used to have us say for a quickie, that she was in a hurry to get us all off to bed quick. [This "quickie" was a shorthand form of "The Lord's Prayer," also in Gaelic.]

She'd come upstairs, put the younger ones to bed. But the older ones would go to bed by themselves. But all I can remember is us going around her on our knees in prayer with her. And she'd put her hand on our shoulders, sort of— you know, on our heads. And she'd have a prayer with us. But to come upstairs, no. She didn't have the time, really and truly. Even when we'd go to bed, she'd start to set her bread. Maybe she'd be another hour downstairs doing things.

And sometimes, Papa'd say books—that's what we'd call it. He'd read a piece in the Bible, a chapter in the Bible. And then we'd all go on our knees, and Papa'd make a Gaelic prayer. Sometimes Mama'd go and do this to him—[give him a sign]—because he kept on and on and on and on, you know, in prayer. To wake him up, you know. "That's enough." Because we'd be starting to wiggle, you know, and giggle, and tickling one another. And she knew that we were getting itchy…. And Papa'd go into his prayer for so long.

And then, we'd go to bed. We'd say the prayer, our night prayer, with Mama. And we'd go up to bed. Then we'd get up in the morning, and the first thing, we'd get out of bed—honest, it was really, truly wonderful. I'd get out of bed. And we'd go on our knees, and we'd say that quick prayer that she taught us. And then we'd

get dressed and come downstairs, and do our duties, washing. And she'd have breakfast ready. We'd all sit at the table.

And then, there was a grace said at the table. And we'd eat—we'd be all through— there'd be a grace said at the table. And then we'd push back, everybody sit around. Papa'd read a piece of the Bible. And we'd all go on our knees again. But Mama'd generally say, *"Dean goirid e."* That meant, "Make it short"!

(*This scene—it's time for your mother to put the children to bed.*) She'd sit in the rocking chair.... And to this day, I repeat it. And I say my prayers every morning, every night. (*With your mother, that wasn't just a now-and-then thing.*) Oh, every day, every day....

Josie with three of her sisters. Left to right: Kitty, Bena, Annie, and Josie

We were never dressed "to a tea." My mother made our clothes. And she wasn't the only one—all the people on the North Shore. And they made some of our clothes in the loom. She'd make skirts for us. Jackets. And she'd make the *clò* [heavier woolen cloth]—when they go milling? Well then, that stuff there. She used to make the pants—they were much heavier, and warm. And whether it rained or snowed, it didn't go in.

Oh, my God, when I think of those things. But it was fun. Peggy Thomais MacDonald, she was a seamster—is that what you call it? She was great on making—she'd fix a dress for us girls. There was Janie Urquhart and Josie MacDonald and me. We were of the same age and we were always together. And she'd fix up, maybe—I'd have a dress on my mother made. And she wouldn't like how the neck was or something. So she'd get a little piece of white cloth, you know. And she'd cut it out and sew it up, and she'd make a collar to put on it for me. And oh, that was so wonderful.

(*I'd like to know how your mother prepared you as a young girl, for womanhood.*) Well really and truly, telling you the honest truth, none of them prepared the daughters very much. My mother didn't. But I had—well, Peggy Thomais—she was my mother, really. And she prepared her daughter, and me, and Janie Urquhart. The three of us together. She gave us a little lecture about everything.... And it was really great. It was really great.

Of course, see, I had sisters older than me, too. And that helped some. If there was anything came up, you know, we could go and—if we were ashamed to go to my mother, you know, we could ask our older sisters. Whether we got the right answer or not, but we did. But we'd always go to Peggy. Always go and ask her. She was left with five children, very young—very, very young. She had two girls and three boys. And she stayed young. She really did stay young. We girls were starting to grow older. And she never grew older in her mind, she stayed young with us. And she was really great....

(*What about dances? Were there a lot of dances on the North Shore?*) No. There were a lot of milling frolics, an awful lot of milling frolics. Because they'd have to mill the cloth that they'd make—the *clò*—the homespun, and the blankets.... (*So dancing wasn't encouraged?*) No. The only dancing there would be—have dances in Peggy Thomais's barn. There'd be a bunch of us in the wintertime. Not in the summertime, there wouldn't be any. We would be dead before you could—we'd be working up until nine o'clock, really. Anyway, in the wintertime we'd congregate there, boys and girls....

(When we say that Peggy Thomais stayed young, what do we mean?) We mean—is—she didn't seem to grow old like my mother did. My mother had a husband. Well, Peggy Thomais seemed to stay young with her five children. And all us girls were going there all the time. And we were always, all us girls stayed with her. We'd go visiting her all the time. Her house was full of people all the time. And she stayed young.

(*Do you think being a young widow helped them stay young?*) I think so. I really do. (*Try to tell me why.*) Well, the only thing I can think of is that they stayed young because they were with young people....

(*That's an interesting question, whether taking care of a husband can take a lot out of a person.*) [At this idea, Josie laughs.] Well, I guess what that would mean to me, it would be, she'd give her attention to her husband more, and not so much to the children. She was there for the children, but she'd go out to work with her husband more, and all that. But with this Peggy, she'd go for walks with us, she'd do things with us. And she was a seamster—she made clothes. People'd bring a cloth to do, you know, yards of cloth, and make a dress, a suit, or whatever. So like that. And she'd go with us. And she'd go swimming with us. You know, that kind. Well, my mother didn't. She had too much to do, probably, or something. I don't know. Or she didn't have that youth. (*She had more of a man's sched-*

ule, too.) Yeah. She'd be working with my father more....

Papa, he used to go to the barn in Breton Cove—when the crowd was around, you know—he couldn't pray in the house by himself. And he'd go to the barn. And he used to forget that he was praying. And we could hear him at the house, he'd be praying so loud.

We didn't think anything of it, you know, because we heard him. And we heard the prayers so many times. (*He did that every night?*) Oh, yeah. (*He'd go up to the barn, every night, and pray?*) Yeah. We often—well, the three of us girls, we used to talk quite a bit up in the States. We could even stop, and we could hear him. (*When you were living in the States.*) Yeah, you know, we heard it so many times, you know, that it was in our.... I don't know.

Anyway, maybe in the afternoon we'd be sitting talking. And we'd say something. "*A bheil thu cluint e?*"—"Are you hearing him?" we'd say. And we'd look at one another, you know. And you could stop there—and you could almost hear him.

Peggy Thomais MacDonald
with her mother Catherine

A North Shore Sabbath

DAN CAMERON, *Aspy Bay*: When North River Lumber Company was working, there wasn't a man went to Maine or New Brunswick or anything. They all—from here [northern Cape Breton], or from Margaree or Chéticamp, or the North Shore—they worked in North River. Tarbot—there were a lot of fellows in Tarbot I knew. I knew an awful lot of the fellows on the North Shore.

(*There was a group of you travelling together?*) Well, at that time the *Aspy*—she came here twice a week, from Sydney right to Bay St. Lawrence. Freight and passengers. And to get on the *Aspy*, you'd go as far as Ingonish. Get off there. The next day, the *Aspy* was coming down to Breton Cove. She'd go into Sydney and return—get her load—and come down to Breton Cove. Well, all we done was walk from Ingonish, South Ingonish, over Smokey to Breton Cove. And the next day get on the *Aspy*, and she was going in to North River. Right in to the wharf.

(*Sometimes, I guess, people would walk all the way.*) Oh, yes, in the spring of the year, or the like of that, before the boat would begin running—no other way. I walked it, good many a time. (*What would you be carrying?*) Well, you wouldn't carry anything. You were coming back—you might have a little light pack. Couple of times, you'd just have a little light pack. But if it was in the spring, you'd have maybe a heavier pack, and you'd have it into a packsack, and put a tag on it, and put it down into the house at the wharf. And it was shipped—they put it aboard the *Aspy*, and it'd land in Dingwall. (*When she'd make her first trip.*) Oh yeah, that's it. (*But you'd walk.*) Yeah. Well, maybe you'd have to wait there two days before the *Aspy*

would come. And—well, you'd be home!

(*That's a long walk.*) Around 50 mile. (*You'd go up there with a crew.*) Yeah. (*Two or three together.*) Oh yes. (*Going at a clip.*) Well that's the only way to get there. There were a lot of fellows go, from Ingonish and Bay St. Lawrence, White Point, Neil's Harbour—going for the drive.

[Coming] from North River, or the drive, or whatever you were coming from—if you'd have a little pack on your back, they didn't want you travelling on the road, on Sunday, carrying a little pack. Now that's a fact.

(*They didn't mind if you walked.*) No. But not carrying anything. (*Going down the North Shore?*) It's a difference. Now, today, you'd go up there, you'd see them up on a roof of a building, shingling. See, now, the way it changed. See people working on a house, on Sunday. And in my time, you couldn't travel the roads carrying a little pack. They were right dead against it.

(*You were telling me that when you walked on the North Shore, you often stayed on the North Shore.*) Oh yes, dozens of times I stayed on the North Shore. (*What happened to you one Sabbath?*) Well, they were Smiths. Just about a mile or a mile and a half on this side of Breton Cove.

A North Shore Sabbath

They lived on the left-hand side if you come this way. It was a fine evening, and I kept on travelling, till it got a little dusky, before I made my mind up to look for a place to stay. I saw this house—nice-looking house—and I went up and rapped on the door.

An old lady come to the door—oh, she wasn't old—she'd be 70, maybe, 75. And I told her my name, and I was working in the woods, and I was wondering could I get a place to stay for the night. "Oh," she said, "yes. Come on in." Her husband was living—very nice old man—quite old. And her son—just the three of them.

I was good and hungry, too. And I remember she got supper for me, and she had good tea and Scotch cake, you know—bannock—the old people called it. That was the Scotch cake. And rhubarb that she put up in the summer—it was in bottles—and cream, good butter. And that tasted good, real good.

So the next day was Sunday. (*They gave you a room to sleep.*) Oh yes, yes, yes. I did have a small little pack. And the old gentleman said to

me—he noticed me getting underway, you know. "Oh," he said, "are you carrying anything?" I said, "I've got a little small pack." "Well," he said, "we don't allow anyone here to travel the road on Sunday and carry anything, pack on your back." He said, "We don't allow it." "So," he said, "now, you're comfortable here, you're welcome to stay, and wait till tomorrow morning."

So I couldn't argue against him. I stayed. And we talked—it was great to talk. And he had his prayers in the night before he went to bed, read the Bible, in the morning. And he wouldn't take a cent. I wanted right away to pay—he said, "No, no." They were fine people on the North Shore. Kind people. Hospitality. And they were good.

(*You would just take a chance on a house.*) Yeah. (*It wasn't that you knew the people.*) Oh no, no, no.

(*And was there any difficulty about the fact that you were Catholic and they were Presbyterian or Protestant?*) No, no.

Men working for the North River Lumber Co. in 1905

With Jack Sam Hinkley of Pleasant Bay

I'LL TELL YOU ABOUT A FELLOW one time got in contact with a bear.

There was a man down here, down in the lower part of the settlement here—a bear came and killed his pig. And they set a gun. Ever hear about setting a gun for an animal? They fix a gun up—make a house and put a gun into it—aimed about the height a bear would be—his breast, you know. And then they had an old muzzle loader—balls in her, I suppose—and they had a string from the trigger of the gun and they had a bait tied to the string. When the bear'd come in and give a jerk on the bait, he'd put the gun off and kill him.

Anyway, the bear came in in the middle of the night—and the gun went off and it hit him in the hip—broke his hip. Well, there was a bunch went down. And there was a man down here, Sandy Moore, a big husky man, and he was scared of nothing—not even scared of a bear. A fellow had a gun there. The bear was up on the hill and he was going to shoot the bear. And Sandy Moore said, "No, no, don't shoot him at all—I'm going to kill him with my bare hands. I read in a book, a magazine," he said, "where an Indian tackled a bear. He killed him with his bare hands. Said he got his hand in his mouth and choked him by the tongue—and I'm going to try it."

So he did. He went after the bear. He had a little stick and he hit the bear on the nose and this made him mad and when he opened his mouth Sandy Moore drove his hand in to about the wrist and he got the tongue and the bear got him by the wrist and away they went, down the mountain, the two of them, end over end. And this is true because there was a man there when it happened told me, and he wasn't lying. Alex Timmons.

Down the mountain they went. And they

couldn't shoot the bear. They were frightened they'd shoot Sandy Moore. And the bear chawed him on the legs and arms, chawed him real bad. And there was a Fraser fellow—Duncan Fraser—he had a great big stone and watched his chance and he struck the bear on the side of the head and he kind of knocked him out—and they got Sandy Moore clear of him.

Now wasn't that a terrible trick for a man to do? And that's a true story.

I ran the mail to Chéticamp with dogs. I mushed her with snowshoes and dog team when there was no road. Only a little trail. In the summertime I used a horse, horseback—the trail wouldn't be cut out any more than six or seven feet. Not that. In the winter with dog team and snowshoes. Dog sleigh. Oh, yes. I had most Newfoundland dogs. I had one Great Dane, female, around 88 or 85 pounds. I had five dogs, I think. Always had a spare one in case there was something wrong with one. Generally only take four. The first years I ran it all the way through from Red River to Chéticamp. Then the last two years I ran it halfway—a Frenchman from Chéticamp would meet me with the mail and take my mail the other way. He'd have two of my dogs and I'd have the other two—and then I could be home every night. I ran twice a week. I started on the first of April in 1919 and I ran it till the last of July in 1923.

Spring—that's the worst time of the year. Half the road would be bare and half snow on it. It was hard for the dogs to haul the mail. And you couldn't get through it with a horse or anything. The month of April was the worst month of the year. The month of April and the month of December I found the two worst months. December days were short and the weather was dark and overcast and snowing all the time in December. Three o'clock it's coming dark some days. And it'd get dirty.

I was out in a snowstorm it was snowing a foot an hour. Made it—but that was all. You couldn't stop, once you were on that road—you had to keep going. There wasn't a farm between here and Cape Rouge.

I stayed at Aucoin's. Oh, I had a nice place to stay. Nice clean bed to sleep in and plenty good food. Aw, they were lovely people. Makes me lonely going by that Cape Rouge yet—they're all gone out of there. Park [Cape Breton Highlands National Park] drove them out.

Anyway, I'd come back fresh the next day. Walked on snowshoes. The dogs when it was good going on the grade, I'd ride on the load—but most of the time I walked. Lots of times I had to break a road ahead of the dogs with the snowshoes. And when crust was on it I'd have to have a shovel and sometimes shovel a path for me and the dogs to get through.

And summertime on horseback and these corduroy bridges—you know, poles laid on the mud—maybe the poles would be broken—well, if he'd go down two feet in that you'd think you were never coming out of it if you were on his back.

But I liked it all right. Yeah. I wish I was smart enough to do it again. I'm going on ninety. I was born February 19, 1888.

Jerome Mountain, at Cap Rouge, was a formidable opponent to early automobiles and their drivers. Johnny Roach remembers being summoned to the aid of drivers who froze at the wheel while trying to negotiate the road over the mountain, in which cases the nervous driver would slide into a passenger seat while the amused Johnny guided the car safely down the hill. Connected with this, he reminisces that "The most peculiar thing I have ever seen was two men and two women going up Cap Rouge Mountain. One woman was running ahead of the car to see the curves, and there were two men running behind the car with big rocks in their hands in case the car stalled [and began to roll backwards]." – from Judith V. Campbell's *Report of the Human History of Cape Breton Highlands National Park*

La Chandeleur— a Feast of the Candles

MARGUERITE GALLANT, *La Pointe:* And something else they used to celebrate which they don't now is something they called the *Chandeleur*, when they bless the candles. Oh, it used to be a great feast. You should have seen what they called *la cane de la Chandeleur*—it was a big staff—oh, it must have been about eight feet. And it had a crook in it. And the man that carried that cane was in full dress, and in the olden time they had shoes—they used to call them little red-topped boots—it had a sort of heart design. It would be handmade, the red top. It was beautiful, more like chamois. He had on an evening coat, a split-tailed coat and everything. And a lovely handmade shirt. Oh, I remember the beautiful linen they used to weave on the loom. And there was a song we'd sing:

> *Nous sommes les gens de la Chandeleur*
> *Si vous voulez nous donner de quoi*
> *Si vous fournissez vous y viendrez*
> *Si vous fournissez pas vous viendra pas.*

There were all kinds of songs and dances. It was a kind of an Indian song and a kind of Russian dance: first they'd go and tap their feet, and after their knee down and their backside down on the ground. And the man there would have his cane all decorated with ribbons and lace, and there would be eyes you'd put the ribbon through and make a bow knot.

And for the *Chandeleur*—they used to have two or three carts, and every house they went maybe one would give a chicken, one give a great big chunk of meat, maybe somebody would give a whole lot of flour and raisins and lard and what have you. And then they'd take that to the lower end of the island there—Chéticamp Island—to a big house. And they'd cook it there. And as long as there was food there they'd eat and drink and dance.

JOE DELANEY, *St. Joseph du Moine*: Take the *Chandeleur* my brother and I were playing down there at Marcellin Charlo Doucet's at Ruisseau du Lac in about 1934. That was one of the last ones in the district. We were playing violin. We started at three in the afternoon and we finished the next day at 11:30 in the morning.

At that time nobody'd hire you. What they used to do, about four times during the night they'd pass the hat, taking up a collection for the fiddlers. We were on the kitchen table playing—and all you had was a break for supper and a break for lunch and a break for breakfast—and then somebody'd be after you, "Come on let's go. Let's get the music going." Well, you didn't want to refuse.

Well anyway they took us up four collections during the night and between the two of us it amounted to 14 dollars and 40 cents. So it gave us 7 dollars and 20 cents for having played for about 19 hours you might as well say. There was no money at the time. But all the treats and the hospitality—you know, the friendship that reigned—look, you would have played for nothing.

I mean, you saw that everybody was so satisfied. Because—let's take it from when the dance first opened—three o'clock—there were no teenagers there—all parents, fathers and mothers, elderlies—and the way it started off is with a French Four. There'd be two men and two women. It was a fast tune, and they would be around 60 years of age—and it was something pretty to look at, to see those two men and those two women working away. They'd step for a while standing one opposite the other—the four on the floor—then all of a sudden they'd start going around accompanying the music—and then they'd stop again and drive her again at stepping. You'd get the four best ones on the floor and look, everybody'd be looking at them. And to play for them was a pleasure, you enjoyed so much to see them dance—especially at that age.

And the other one—they used to call them in French *Une Huit*—An Eight—something similar to the square sets they dance today but there's a difference. And the ones that could dance those Eights—they'd get almost the best there—four couples. Well, listen here. Boy, everybody did their part so well, and they were stepping away also. It was something beautiful to look at. They don't have anything today like that. No banquet to compare or wedding festivities to compare to what that had. This was a community spirit, a community festival—this thing. And everybody pitched in. Everybody wanted to make sure that it went over good. It's too bad, too bad, that it did come to an end.

MARGUERITE GALLANT: The festival of *Chandeleur* used to start before the second of February, because Lent would generally begin there. Not always, but when it did they'd make sure that Lent wasn't going to bother them—they had to plan their holidays. For a week they wouldn't do anything else, they wouldn't go to the woods—generally they would be all through with chopping wood, hauling it and sawing it. They'd go fishing for smelts and they'd go hunting for seals—oh, it was great sport in the olden times. Now the people are too lazy. And now they have to be paid no matter what it is. They used to work work work like slaves for nothing. Now to work for nothing is no pleasure for anybody. They would work two or three for one man, two or three for another man, until all the work was done. Then, *Chandeleur*.

JOE DELANEY: The first thing you had to do you had to go and visit somebody if they'd be willing to give their house for the *Chandeleur*. By giv-

ing the house that didn't mean they were only going to use the kitchen and the front room. In St. Joseph du Moine alone there were 55 families and a lot of people home at that time. When you gave your house for the population it was going to serve, well the upstairs was just as busy as the downstairs. There'd be 10 or 12 in one room and 15 in another—and they'd be talking and drinking and having a great time. So the first thing was to get someone to donate his house—and you had a hard time because it's not everyone who wanted to give his house. There'd be many reasons. Somebody would probably have an elderly person who wasn't feeling too well. And one would have given his house but his house was too small. You generally went to the biggest houses.

Then on the last of January and on the first of February, generally on the first of February—the younger men would get together. They'd use sleighs for hauling wood and they'd have an open box on it. And in there they'd have a tub for meat and containers for flour, sugar, salt, potatoes, carrots and everything. There'd be about three sleighs covering the district and they'd go to every house and everybody would go in and they had what they called *la cane de la Chandeleur.* That was your leader. Well this cane was all decorated with ribbons up on top. And the people were expecting you because they knew you were gathering the grub to be cooked the night before and the morning of the *Chandeleur.* And you had a dance that they called *L'Escaouette*—the leader up front with his cane and you were dancing in a circle going around in the kitchen [each with his hands on the shoulders of the one in front, beating time]—and when it came to the chorus of the song, then you'd start stepping away.

L'Escaouette

C'est monsieur l'marié et madam' marié' [bis]
C'est monsieur, madam' mariés [bis]
Qu'ont pas encor soupé. [bis]
Un p'tit moulin sur la rivière,
Un p'tit moulin pour passer l'eau.
Le feu sur la montain, boy run, boy run,

Le feu sur la montain, boy run away.
J'ai vu le loup, le r'nard, le lièvre,
J'ai vu la grand' cité sauter,
J'ai foulé ma couvert', couvert', vert', vert'.
J'ai foulee ma couvert', couverte aux pieds.
Aouenne, aouenn', guenille,
Ah! rescou' ta guenille,
Aouenne, aouenne, aouenne, nippaillon!
Ah! rescou' tes brillons.
Tibounich, nabet, nabette!
Tibounich, naba!

Then once the song was over the people'd give us the food—whatever they wanted to donate—you accepted everything. And once you had everything gathered you finished off by thanking the people with a song: *"En vous remerciant, mes gens d'honneur d'avoir fourni pour La Chandeleur. Un jour viendra Dieu vous l' rendra. Alleluia."* "We thank you very much folks for having contributed to the *Chandeleur.* One day will come, God will bless and reward you. Halleluia."

In every house it was the same ceremony. And every time your sleigh was loaded you'd take it up to the house [where they'd hold the party]. And the next move was to get the ladies of the district—about 10 or 12 of them—to assist the woman of the house—for peeling potatoes, peeling turnips and all that. Some ladies would take home a pot of meat. There wasn't enough room to cook everything at one house.

Just to give you an idea—February second—we got into there at three in the afternoon down at Marcellin Doucet's. That was one of the last ones in the district done in the old way. My brother Arthur and I were playing the violin. Those were the Hungry 'Thirties, Mister, and times were hard. We left with each our fiddle, and for our cases we had a white pillow case. We landed there at three o'clock. They were waiting for us to get the dance going. So we danced till about 5:30 and then we stopped for supper. It would only be for the parents—the head of the households. The teenagers would be arriving about seven to dance. As it was they were serving 75 to 110 people. And you didn't stop playing the violin for the whole of the supper. We were the first table to eat. And listen here, at that time, when you went to a place like that, and once you entered the dining room and saw that table—well listen here that would make your eyes open, Mister, twice as big as what they were. It was the Depression, and let me tell you that tables loaded with food the way these *Chandeleur* were presented—to see the food that was on there! Well, they'd take off the potatoes and the meat, parsnips, carrots, chow, turnips and all the rest and then they'd come on with the pastry: pies, cookies, cakes, donuts—homemade donuts—well listen here, were you ever full!

Quarter to seven then get started back on the violin. Till about 11, 11:30. Then there was another big lunch: meat sandwiches and sweets of all kinds but the meat sandwiches were the ones you'd go for. Why? Because at a party like that—at that time you didn't talk about going to the liquor store. Everybody knew that this *Chandeleur* was coming. Everybody would get a gallon of molasses, you know, and make his own home brew. Molasses, yeast cake, and water—that would only take you about a week to get a five-gallon keg. Others made their beer in December and they distilled it for moonshine. And some thoughtful residents had made some homemade wine for the ladies: beet wine, blueberry wine, and another they used to call *chaspareille* which had a good kick in it. Mister, all the stuff to drink!

This big lunch and you'd stop for an hour and get right back at it. 'Round 12:30 the dance would continue. They were dancing in two rooms—one set in one room and one set in the other—and drive 'er MacIver. This went on till 5:30, but about one o'clock some of the elderlies would start leaving—but some of them were going home to get a few hours sleep in order to get back there about half past six in the morning. We played till half past five and then stopped for breakfast. And after having been on home brew and moonshine for almost 16 hours—just because we had come there to play you were offered more treats—well sometimes you had to refuse because we had been asked to play and you had to watch out not to pass out. Anyway for breakfast you didn't care for sweets, eh? You weren't too fussy about pastry and preserves. You wanted something salty. And what did they have on the menu? Potatoes and pickled mackerel. Well does that ever hit the spot.

And now the old-timers who had gone home were coming back because they were saying to themselves, "At home we might get preserves." And after breakfast again the dance would go on till about 11:30—then everybody would head for home.

MARGUERITE GALLANT: You know that *Chandeleur* I believe was an Indian holiday. I kind of think so. The song they used to sing: *Aouenne, aouenne*—it was supposed to be an Indian song. You know here in Chéticamp there was an awful lot of Indians when they first came. Living on the beach here. And there was some kind of village over there on the island. When you plow you find—well, yes, I found some arrowheads in my garden—but where the camps were you find oyster shells, a foot or more of oyster shells—they would plow through that. Then the French people came and the Jersey people—they used to celebrate that. They called it the *Chandeleur*—that's because it's the second of February—that's the day the blessed candles used to be blessed.

And they *are* blessed, if you have faith. They are used if there's a big storm, a bit southeast. Whether it does good or bad, it's faith. Some do it still. You get the candles from the church. You light these candles whenever you're sick, when you're going to be prepared for death. I have faith in those things; I think that's what they're blessed for.

If you have no faith you're not fit to live. That is the best way to express myself. And at the feast of Pentecost and Holy Saturday they bless the holy water. You know they use it for baptism and they use it for sacramental work. And then the other holy water is blessed for the land and the sea. You know, when I make my garden I'm going to spray a whole lot of holy water in it.

MARIE (MRS. WILLIE D.) DEVEAU, *Belle Marche*: They are blessing the candles yet but we go and get them from the priest. In those days they used to make candles. Not everybody, but whoever did would make some for the neighbourhood. Like an old lady who was right by where we were living. She used to make candles. She had molds. You know, and she used to melt tallow—it wasn't bee's wax then. They would take the candles to the church to be blessed on the second of February. We used to have a lot of confidence in them—more than the young people—when it was thundering, lightning and things like that—well, we used to light the candles for God to preserve us. It was better than cursing, eh? And the holy water—we used to go around the house and make a cross on all the windows. Well, the old people had faith in that. But listen, if you have no faith in it, it's no use to do it. Well, I *do* have faith in it but I don't do it. I pray. Say if I was scared, I'd pray. Maybe I would light a candle if I was scared. It depends on how scared you are.

JOE DELANEY: And in those days also people would go to the church in the morning to get their throats blessed. The priest at the altar had two candles—the candles of St. Blaize—and they were crossed and caught together. There would be one on each side of your throat. The candle would be straight coming at you and then it was turned up on each side of your throat. And these candles were lit. And a lot of people wouldn't miss mass that morning—to get their throat blessed. They also blessed the candles that morning and everybody was given two. It was a yearly event.

Two tourists in 1935, trying to negotiate Jerome Mountain at Cap Rouge: "Oh, a horse and buggy coming! What in the world shall we do? The horse is skittish. Dan puts on both brakes. They hold us in mid-air. The man gets out and runs to the horse's head. A young mother, holding a little child, looks up at us out of eyes wide with apprehension. Mercifully there are a few extra feet of siding. The man leads his horse gently out of the middle way and holds him as Dan lets in the clutch and inches Sally [their car] past so quietly that the horse does not plunge." – from Gordon Brinley's *Away to Cape Breton*

Kenneth MacKenzie, Margaree

MY GRANDMOTHER was a MacLean. They had had to change their names from MacGregor to MacLean because MacGregors were outlawed in Scotland at that time—so she happened to come here as a MacLean. And I remember her. She was 102, I think, when she died. And her cheeks were as red—when she was over 100. And she had all her teeth. And they told me that she grew a tooth when she was something over 70. And she had a son who had a double set of teeth. And he never lost a tooth, and he was 85 when he died.

But my grandfather—I'll tell you this. Years ago, my grandfather, he was quite a man to swear. Although he was a Presbyterian. But there was one woman, she was very, very religious—and she was bedridden. And she was in a bed right off of the kitchen. And my grandfather went in the house one day and he sat down at the stove, and I guess the language he was using was terrible. And she chastized him for swearing.

"Well," he said, "if you had the same thing wrong with you that I got"—remember, she was bedridden; but he considered his ailment worse. He said, "If you had the same thing wrong with you, you'd be swearing, too."

"Well," she said, "what's wrong?" He said he had a toothache. She said, "Well, if I could get to where I'd want to go with you, I'd cure your toothache." He said, "Where do you want to go?" So she described the place. It was a spring up in the side of a hill, in the side of the mountain, up in the Big Intervale there. And they could see it from where they were.

Well anyway, he said, "I'll see that you get up there."

So it was all feather beds they had. He went home and he took one of those ticks off the bed, and he emptied the feathers out of it and went and put her in this tick, and carried her up the mountain where she wanted to go. And she went through whatever ritual it was—I *did* hear it. It was a prayer that she said, and he had to say it too—and it was in Gaelic they were saying it. And he took a mouthful of water and said a prayer, and she scooped up a sod or he scooped it up, and he spit under the sod and put the sod back.

Well, his toothache disappeared.

But a few years afterward, my mother came home, just before I was born. And she had a toothache. And she wasn't too old at the time, and she complained of this toothache, and my grandfather told her this story about the old lady curing his toothache. She said, "I wish the old lady was here now"—she had died. "Well," he said, "I remember exactly what she did. If you want to go and try it, we'll go."

Well, they went up. I remember my mother talking about it. They had to cross the river on horseback, and she fell off right in the middle of the river. But anyhow, they got up to this spring and they went through the same performance as this old lady did. My mother never had a toothache again. And I've never had a toothache in my life. I don't know what toothache means.

And my mother—when she was older—sat on a chair in the kitchen there, and the doctor came and pulled, I think, fifteen teeth, and she didn't even have it frozen. She was quite old when the doctor pulled her teeth. And I've got teeth broken off right to the gum—and I never had a toothache. And this happened through her. I wasn't born when my grandfather took her up there—that was just before I was born.

(*And they do say that these things have to be transmitted from a man to a woman....*)

And from a woman to a man. But those old fellows that came from Scotland, they all had that. And I've often heard the old fellows talking about this same woman—this woman was a MacPherson. All I ever heard them call her was Widow MacPherson. You know, there'd be kids around, and a fellow would get a piece of bark or something in his eye—and then the kids would run up to this old lady and tell her that a certain person had something in his eye. She'd go through some kind of a ritual—the person would probably be miles away—and she'd come up with that piece of bark. They used to say she'd take a cup of water—but nobody knew just what she did—nobody ever saw. She'd go in her room.

Now we were talking about spearing salmon. There was a MacLean woman up there—she had two sons—and her husband was dead for a number of years, and they were having quite a struggle to get along. And they were peeling birchbark—that's what they used to use under shingles, was birchbark—I think they used to get a cent a sheet for it in Chéticamp. So she and the two boys went out and they peeled a lot of this bark, and they hid it in this old Widow MacPherson's house—they didn't hide it, they stored it there. And they had it piled in probably the kitchen, I don't know. And the way they had it weighted down was boards on top and big rocks to keep it flat.

And sometime through the summer, the river filled up with salmon—they had a freshet and salmon came in. And my Uncle Rod and a Murray fellow decided to go get some salmon, but they needed something to make a light [to spear salmon at night]. And the only thing they could think of was this birchbark. They decided that if they go and take the bark and pay her for it, she won't have to carry it to Chéticamp.

So they went up to this house, nice sunny afternoon—and they couldn't take a board off of that pile of birchbark. They said, when they'd touch it the house would shake and you'd think there was a thousand horses galloping around outside. So they didn't take the bark. And they weren't stealing it. They were figuring on paying her for it. But it was well-protected—by something.

They believed very much in witches, in the old country, the old fellows here talked. (*Any talk of witches in the Margaree Valley?*) No. Well, yes, there was an old woman up the Big Intervale there, and a bunch of them were watching her one day, and she threw a chip in the river and jumped on it and crossed over. But I never heard too much of that. Because my folks didn't believe in that sort of thing. (*But you wouldn't consider Widow MacPherson a witch?*) Oh, no. They figured what she had, it was more a gift. It was a gift.

And the same woman, I've heard my grandmother say, there was a MacLeod, a little kid—she used to take epileptic fits—and they got Widow MacPherson. And my grandmother said that she was there with her—she used to take somebody with her, you know, to drive a horse. And she went into this house and asked them where the kid fell for the first fall that she had. And she got a chicken—and I guess it had to be a black chicken—and she took the chicken and put it on her hand and stroked it a few times. And whether she mesmerized it or hypnotized it—anyway, the chicken went to sleep. So she took the chicken and buried it in the basement underneath where the kid fell. The child never had another fit.

Archie Neil Chisholm, Margaree Forks

SADDLED WITH POLIO, pride, and a lack of discipline, Archie Neil Chisholm lived out the contradictory life of a terrific schoolteacher floundering in alcoholism. He emerged as an extraordinarily valuable person in the Cape Breton community—as storyteller, master-of-ceremonies, teacher, of course, and friend.

I GOT WORD OF PAPA'S DEATH while I was correcting student papers at Belle Côte. I was boarding with Bill and Mary Matheson. They came to my room and I knew what they were going to tell me. It was strange but earlier a group of friends came by to ask me to play at a wedding, and I said, "No, my father is sick, and I don't think I should go." But I didn't know he was so close to the end.

The first thought I had when I stood at the foot of Papa's bed was that I had disappointed him, and now there was no way to change that.

After the prayers at the gravesite, Father Cormier held Momma's hands and looked directly into her face. She was blind now, and deaf. He knew that she had not heard a word of the church service. He spoke very loud, in part saying, "*Cridhe glan soluis am broilleach a leine.*" He had carefully learned and rehearsed the old saying especially for her. "He had a pure heart of light in the bosom of his shirt."

What made me cry was being a disappointment to Papa. I knew what he wanted for me, and instead of doing something about it, I got to the point where I used to come home in pretty bad shape at times.

Now this is as it actually happened.

One particular night a friend of mine and I were driving home, and he dropped me off at my house. And I managed to get into the house all right. But the next day I met him, and he asked me a rather strange question. He asked

me, "Who was the chap who walked in from the gate to the front door of your house last night?"

I laughed at him, because I figured he was putting me on. And he described a man—tall, and dressed in a certain way—which immediately struck me as being the identical image of my father, who was then dead, had passed away. I figured that possibly he was just making this up.

But on three different occasions other people had told me that they were seeing this particular man walking with me whenever I would leave a car. And it was particularly in the wintertime.

So one night I came into my own house, and my two brothers were in the living room. One of my brothers opened the door for me, and looked over my shoulder, and didn't say anything. But the next morning he told me that my father had followed me in to the door, that he was positive that he recognized him. This I again assumed to be a ploy to try to scare me into not drinking any more.

But time went on, a year or so after that. I was at a dance, a place called Chéticamp. And we left Chéticamp in a very bad storm. And I got home to my own driveway. I got out of the car. I started in to the house, home. My last recollection was of sort of falling down in the snow. And I made no attempt whatsoever to get up.

But somehow during the night my brother woke up, and he woke his wife up, and he said, "Archie Neil is someplace out there." And he came out, and he picked me up. And without his assistance I would have died that night.

I didn't speak very much about it for a couple of days afterward, and then I asked him. I said, "Rod, how is it that you were able to come out and find me at three o'clock in the morning in a snowstorm when you were supposedly sound asleep?"

And he looked at me for a moment, and then he said, "Well, if I tell you, you won't believe me." I said, "Yes, I will." He said, "Our father appeared at the side of my bed and told me that you were out there, and I went out." And he said, "Otherwise, you would have been dead."

So, a few things happening like that made me decide that I was through with drinking….

No, actually, that wasn't it.

What made me decide to drop it was the fact that I was on an Easter safari with a group of people, and I came home to my boarding house. I was boarding at St. Joseph du Moine. I left school on Easter Thursday evening. And that was in the days when they had a full week. I hadn't taken a drink for quite a few weeks. And I decided, I've just got to have it—no more school for seven or eight days.

So I went on a bad one. And I was travelling around with the same guy all the time. We weren't sleeping. We were just going from house to house, bootlegger to bootlegger, liquor store or anything. And I came home and I was broke. I didn't come home—I went to my boarding house—and the man with whom I was boarding said, "Archie Neil, come on in the house. You're in pretty bad shape."

And I said, "I know, Thomas." I said, "I won't. I don't want your wife, Adèle, to see me like this."

And Thomas said, "Adèle—you have her worried worse than your mother. She sees you going by, and she likes you. And she said you've never done anything in the house, or said anything that was out of the way. You've always managed to get to your room. Come on in. I'll tell you what I'll do. If you will stay home, I'll get you two quarts."

I went up to the house, and I said hello to Adèle. I was able to walk, navigating okay with a cane, just a cane. I had dispensed with the crutches in 1927 and started using the cane. And I got that I could walk very well with it. And the idea was to get me off the road. By gosh, he brought the two quarts up to my room. And I said, "I'm broke, Thomas." I said, "I'll pay you when I come out of this."

And I started to drink alone.

I had a couple of bottles of rum, and I was drinking alone in my bedroom. All of a sudden I put my hand in my pocket—they had a little store downstairs, and I was going to get some cigarettes. And I didn't have a cent, not one penny in my pocket. And I thought to myself, Here I am 43 years old, and I've worked since I was 19—and I didn't have the price of a package of cigarettes. And the strangest thing about it was—you may think this is crazy—but I had drunk myself sober rather than drunk. I was drinking, drinking, just all alone, straight out of the bottle. And then all of a sudden this hit me, and I said to myself, "This is it. I'm going to quit."

There was a full quart and a half quart there. And I took the half quart. The window was up, and I threw it out the window, smashed it on the rocks. And Thomas heard the smash, and made for upstairs. He said, "What in the name of God is wrong with you?" I said, "I will never take another drink, Thomas."

And Thomas laughed and said, "I've heard that one before. Well, if you're never going to take another drink, I'm going to take that quart." I said, "No. Leave it there. That's going to be a fight between that quart and me—between us," I said.

And that night—of all the sickness and pain and everything else I went through, that night was the worst I ever went through. You're going to laugh at me and say, "He's making it up." But I'll tell you that that bottle had arms on it. It seemed to reach out to me. And I said to myself, for the first time in my life, I'd say, Archie Neil, you have D.T.'s now—when you see things and all of that. And I was able to rationalize. And I'd do that. I'd just pinch myself—yeah, I'm awake. As there's a Saviour above, I'm telling you the truth.

I'd see snakes. As there's a God above me. There were snakes and everything, and they were coming through the keyhole, and they were getting larger as they were coming through. And I was seeing all sorts of ugly faces around me. Nothing pleasant. The most horrible looking faces. Then when I'd sit up in bed and get my bearings, they seemed to disappear. Then I'd just relax and go back to sleep, and as soon as I would be just dozing asleep, back they'd come again.

So I knew it was a figment of the imagination.

I was alone in the room, alone all the time. They would have come up if I had called them. But I was alone in the room. And Mrs. Deveau would come up now and again to see if I wanted a cup of tea or something. She was a lady I'll never forget. I was in this shape that when she brought me a cup of tea I wouldn't take the tea in front of her. I asked her to put it on the chair. When I went to take the tea I couldn't—my hands were shaking that badly I couldn't.

And I stayed in bed for two days. I wouldn't come down. And when the following Monday came, I was ready to go back to teach. It was right on the hill above them. It was a two-room school then. I went to teach.

And about two weeks or three weeks afterwards, I came downstairs one day with the quart. I had broken the half quart out the window, but I left the full one. I came down and I put it on the table. And I said, "Thomas, I've gotten a cheque and I'm going to pay you." So I paid him for the quart that I drank. And I said, "There's the other one, or I'll pay you for that. What'll you do with it, break it?" "No," he said, "I'll keep it." He looked me straight in the eyes. "For the first time in my life," he said, "I'm believing you."

And so, from that day on I never looked back. No, never.

In 1890, at the Great Falls on Indian Brook, Frank Bolles wrote: "This scene of beauty is a focus of Nature's deepest and purest life; and though in it man has no place, it does not on that account lack meaning or significance. Man is a masterful figure in the drama of creation, but he is not all, nor even half, what the world has long been taught to consider him. Perhaps he has been studied too much. Certainly Nature, unspoiled by his greed, has not been studied enough, or loved enough. Standing in that fair solitude, as much alone as on some atoll in a distant sea, I felt as though I might know man better, see him in stronger contrasts and clearer lights, if I could live apart from him longer in such still, calm, holy places as Indian Brook canyon. —quoted from *From Blomidon to Smoky*

From a Visit with Frank and Margaret MacRae

FRANK MACRAE *of North River Bridge*: I remember, too, we had a fellow by the name of Kenny Mac-Leod over here. And we were at a sawmill. And a bunch of us going—maybe 10 to 12 men—cutting fire-wood [going farm to farm, blocking it up to stove length] with a machine. And this Kenny MacLeod, he had Gaelic and he could read Gaelic. And after dinner, everybody'd flop on the floor down in the dining room, you know, and Kenny would get the book and start reading the stories. That was every year. Every year. Next year again, one would tell Kenny, "Kenny, get the book."

(*You were together cutting wood....*) Yes. From house to house. You know, we were [each] hauling the firewood home during winter. When everyone would have their firewood home, then Donald Garrett out here, he used to have a [por-table] sawmill. And you would have to have maybe from 8 to 12 men chunking it up. That was about a day's work. You'd come in for a cup of tea at 10 o'clock. And then out again, the bunch, and then come in to dinner. Have your big dinner, you know, the best—lots of meat and gravy and potatoes and everything else. Then, if it was a big pile, maybe you'd be there for supper.

But that was the carry-on every year. When Kenny would be with us, indeed you would have the Gaelic book. He'd read that story. Every year.

After dinner. We were having a rest, and every-body smoking. We'd lay on the floor, you know. An hour for dinner. He would get the book and he would sit down. And everybody so interested in those stories.

(*And when you went around doing this work, was there any pay for it?*) Pay? No. Pay—nothing! No, we didn't get anything. But I'll tell you the way it was. A bunch would come here. And then I would have to go with them. Day for day. (*Did you cut anybody's wood, that wasn't among the men doing the work?*) Oh yes, in the neighbourhood. Somebody was sick, you know, we'd all go there and help....

(*When the men were getting together to cut wood from house to house, and you'd have that big dinner, did the women also get together to cook those dinners, or did the one woman of that house prepare it alone?*)

MARGARET MACRAE: One woman of that house did the cooking for that day. Perhaps if we had pickled beef; or if they'd killed a cow, maybe a roast of beef. Or maybe it'd be a big pot of stew. We'd have that. And the turnips and carrots and vegetables. And then we'd have some kind of dessert—maybe cottage pudding or maybe pies, or whatever. Homemade biscuits and bannock and homemade bread.

(*But it wasn't that your friend next door knew they were coming the next day, and she'd help you get that stuff ready.*) No, no. You were doing it. Then they'd know where they were going the next day, and that woman would be preparing for when they'd come to her. You'd have to be prepared [for supper] too, just in case they didn't finish, if something broke down. Perhaps you'd have a pot of beans that you'd cook for supper, or something like that. That you could serve them if it was necessary. Have them in at tea at three o'clock. Maybe they'd be through shortly after that and they'd go home and have their supper at home. Or maybe if something broke down, they'd have to stay and have supper. So you had to be prepared for it all. (*So the men would gather to get the work done efficiently, but the women—each one took care of her own home.*) Yes, that's right.

And the men, there'd be seven or eight or ten men there. They'd come early in the morning. Today they'd be here. Then they'd go to the next house the next day. The same crew went mostly to all the places in this area. Then when you went a little further away, there'd be another crew.

FRANK: Oh, it was a good pastime.

MARGARET: Nobody went to the hospital to have a baby—that was unheard of. All my children were born in the house. But I was lucky I had a doctor and a nurse. But in those days, they had nobody but a granny. No doctor or nurse, just a granny. They never seemed to have complications, you know. It was strange, you know. I never recall them telling the story about how the baby died because there was no attending physician or nurse or anything.

And there was one story that Frank's mother used to tell us. There was a relative of

his father's lived down in Cape North. And this morning she got up in the morning and she decided she was going to come out here to North River to visit them. Started from Cape North walking. And she got here late in the evening. Imagine! From Cape North! (*That would be 62 miles.*) And she wasn't in very long when Frank's mother told her that there was a young woman down the road here about a mile, and she was expecting a baby. And she said, "They've been there all day, and the baby hasn't come yet, and it looks as if they're going to lose the mother. She just can't deliver." "Oh," she said, "we'll have to go there right away. Let's go down to see."

So Frank's mother and herself got ready, and they went down to the house down the road. She went in there where all the neighbours were gathered in there waiting, just expecting the mother to pass out any time. And this old lady, she went in the room. There were several people in the room with the mother, and she said to them, "Now, I want everyone of you to go out of the room. But I want two good strong men to stay." So there were two of the men stayed, and the rest went out. And she said to them, "You get her up on her feet and start making her walk. And make her walk up and down." And they started doing that back and forth. And by gosh, didn't the baby deliver!

She delivered the baby, and she saved the mother's life, she saved the baby's life. And she was saying, "I knew," she said, "that there was something giving speed to my feet when I was coming from Cape North. It was almost as if I was on wings." And she was here in time to deliver that baby and save the mother's life. After walking from Cape North. She was an Urquhart. Elly Urquhart.

(*How long after your own children were born did you stay in bed?*) Oh, maybe a week. Oh, you were allowed to get up, you know, to go use the bathroom or something—but you'd stay in bed. And they used to say it was very important to stay in bed, I think it was on the ninth day or something like that. That was the day that everything was supposed to go back into place inside. That's supposing you had been up the day before, then you should go back to bed that day. I think it was the ninth day.

(*What about preparation beforehand? Were there things you weren't supposed to do?*) No. I was housecleaning. Sandy was born in May, and Kerr was born in May, and I was housecleaning—taking down curtains and putting up curtains and doing all those things. When Kerr was born, I guess it was, I made a wash in the morning, put it out on the line. Annie Mae [Margaret's sister] was going to come out and stay with me. So Frank went to get her that day, down to the Barachois. And there was so much snow on the Barachois that my brother came with a truck as far as the Barachois Bridge, but he couldn't get through the Barachois Mountain. And Frank went down with a horse and wagon and met him there, and took Annie Mae out here.

I had a wash out on the line, and I went out and took it in after Annie Mae came. I had set

bread, and I was starting kneading the bread, and oh, by gosh, I started thinking something was going to happen. And I didn't say anything to them for a while. Of course, if I'd dare mention it to him, he'd be off to get somebody right away. He wouldn't wait to see if it was real or not.

So, anyway. Sure enough. Annie Mae wasn't here very long when I knew that, well, I guess we were going to have to get—I think it was Mrs. Fraser that came up. She was living down at the foot of the hill here, and she was sort of a practical nurse. So Frank went down and got her.

I took the clothes in off the line. You had to have things ready for your bed and all that sort of thing. The doctor came here—he wasn't here more than an hour when the baby was delivered. He was saying to me, "You should have been having the babies for all the women around here!"

Hector Carmichael, St. Ann's, and Alex Kerr, North River Bridge

Alexander Graham Bell Dies at Baddeck

THE END CAME VERY QUICKLY. On August 2, 1922, Mabel cabled to Gilbert Grosvenor, Elsie Bell's husband: "Father died peacefully today. Only within a few days did we realize any danger. I did not send for David and Daisy. They were here by merest chance."

Realizing how distressed Elsie must feel at being so far away, Daisy Bell Fairchild sent her this description of what took place at Beinn Bhreagh:

Alexander Graham Bell and Mabel Bell with their daughters Elsie May (top) and Marian (Daisy), grandchildren, and sons-in-law Gilbert Grosvenor (left) and David Fairchild

"As far as Daddysan was concerned, one could not wish for a more beautiful ending. He was in the porch with the fresh air about him and it was a beautiful moonlight night and not cold. 'How beautiful it is here—the air is so fresh,' he said in the afternoon and he just breathed more deeply and more slowly until finally he didn't breathe again. He pressed Mother's hand almost to the end—and very shortly before he died when Mother was calling him, he opened his eyes and we all knew he had come back and knew her. I am sure Mother told you that—I think it was her greatest comfort.

"I don't think you need fear that Mother will break down now anyway. It makes you cry to see her. She goes on just as usual—makes all the motion—laughs and talks but you never forget for a moment that the heart of everything has gone out of life for her forever.

"She isn't wearing mourning. She says she could never take it off if she did, she couldn't help watching us for the first signs of our putting it off. It would seem like putting off our sorrow. Up here, it has seemed so natural and so beautiful an ending. There was no crepe on the door—no drawn blinds—the children played about and ran up and down stairs—there was no feeling at all that death was terrible.

"The men in the Laboratory made the coffin out of good rugged pine and forged the iron handles. It was lined with aeroplane linen. The children made a pall of green, entirely covered with balsam fir. They cut the branches very short and sewed them on. If you had seen them fitting it over the coffin themselves and doing it so sweetly and seriously, so glad there was something they could do for Grampie, you would be thankful for them that death can never seem a thing to fear.

"The only flowers on the coffin were from the American Tel and Tel Company. The wreath must have been chosen by someone 'with tenderness and imagination' Mother feels. It was made of laurel, sheaves of wheat and pink roses and Mother feels they were chosen—'the laurel for victory, the wheat for the gathered harvest and the roses for gentleness and sweetness.'

"Mother stepped forward and stood alone with her arm resting on the coffin—bare-headed and in white with a soft white scarf around her neck while the Rev. John MacKinnon read a few verses from the 90th Psalm—just the beautiful ones, skipping the

Funeral at Beinn Bhreagh

others. Miss Jean MacDonald sang 'Where Grew a Bonnie Briar Bush' and then played Mendelssohn's funeral march as they carried him out. John was there with the buckboard, the two back seats removed—and Mother, Mabel [Grosvenor] and I with the others behind watched them around the curve. It was a thrilling sight—Casey and Graham [Fairchild] walking at the head of 20 or 30 men—all bareheaded—then John with the buckboard with its fir-covered load.

"Catherine [MacKenzie, A. G. Bell's secretary] drove Mother, Mabel, David, Nancy Bell and me—and the others followed in other cars. Mother had wanted to walk up beside the buckboard but we persuaded her it was too dangerous up the steep part. At the top of the mountain where the road merges from the woods, she got out and walked the rest of the way—David holding her arm. She walked on the right, her left hand on the coffin. Where the road leads straight to the circle, we all got out and followed on foot.

"There were a great many people there. The grave was blasted out of the rock and lined with fir boughs—and there was a steel vault—in case Mother feels she wants Father to go back to America. On the right the American flag and on the left the British were at half mast on short poles. Miss MacDonald sang the verses and we all joined in singing the chorus of 'Bringing in the Sheaves.' Mother watched Miss MacDonald's

face and joined in first of all. Miss MacDonald's voice is beautiful and she sang so that every word was understood. She sang right to Mother. Then she sang Tennyson's 'Crossing the Bar,' then the first verse only of Stevenson's requiem:

> Under the wide and starry sky,
> Dig the grave and let me lie,
> Gladly I lived and gladly I die,
> And I lay me down with a will.

"The music of it is as beautiful as the words and as she sang, we looked over the beautiful stretch of water and hills and sky and it was gray and misty as Father loved it best.

"Mr. MacKinnon read a few words Mother had written explaining that she wanted Longfellow's 'Psalm of Life' read because it typified as could no mere personal words the spirit in which Dr. Bell had lived his life, and then Mr. MacKinnon read it and after that we all said the 'Lord's Prayer' and the coffin was lowered into the grave. 'Lord, now lettest thou thy servant depart in peace. May the peace of God that passeth all understanding be with you and remain with you always, amen.'

"Uncle Charlie [Bell] wonders if any other great man ever had so simple a funeral. I wish you could have been there on the mountain Elsie, darling, and Bert and all your children and everyone who loved Daddysan. It was Mother's planning and Mother's idea that made it like a last message from Daddysan. There was nothing that did not ring absolutely true, there was no presence of any kind, no show.

"I don't believe Mother will ever want Father moved from here. I hope not, but that doesn't need to be decided now—and I know she wants to talk to you. Just now Mother wants to sell the Washington house without ever seeing it again. If Casey can find his life's still here, Mother can go on living here too—going away of course in the winter and keeping the home for us all in the summer. So far there seems no reason why this will not work out...."

Elsie and her mother returned to Washington in December. The doctors examined Mabel and found she was suffering from cancer. For the short time that remained she lived with Daisy. One day near the end, she remarked to her daughter: "Wasn't I clever not to get ill until Daddysan didn't need me any more."

She died on January 3, 1923, at the age of 65, and on August 7, in accordance with her expressed wish, her ashes were placed in her husband's grave on the summit of Beinn Bhreagh. With only the immediate family present, a brief service was conducted by the Reverend John MacKinnon.

The time chosen was five o'clock, the same hour as her husband's funeral a year earlier, the hour at which Mabel was accustomed to joining Alec at the laboratory to drive him home....

From Lilias Toward's biography, *Mabel Bell: Alexander's Silent Partner*.

Minnie Aucoin,
St. Joseph du Moine

A Milling Frolic on the North Shore

THE MILLING FROLIC has played an important role in the survival of Gaelic songs associated with that event. Weaving as a necessity went out as soon as inexpensive factory goods were readily available. The old looms, which took up a room in themselves, went on the rock pile or into the fire—very few were saved—and most of the weavers were grateful to be free of them. But the milling frolic continued in form at least—organized for tourists or for Cape Bretoners home for the summer. An old blanket would be milled over and over, and the community hall would be used instead of a home—but the songs to be heard were as beautiful as ever, and people had a chance to gather together. But we wanted to experience a traditional milling, and in 1978 neighbours along the North Shore set up the one shown here. Josie Tommy MacDonald offered her home and Gwennie Pottie supplied newly woven cloth. Neighbours donated the traditional foods— salt herring, blue potatoes, oatcakes, bannock and strong black tea—and they sang and milled and had a meal in the harrow in a home for the first time since 1939.

JOHN ALEX JOHN X. MACDONALD: You'd hear songs in the homes. Yes. My father was a great singer, and he had a wonderful memory. Everybody talked about him even after he was dead, you know. He'd remember everything. And if he'd go to a milling and hear a song for the first time— he'd sing the whole thing for you the next day, and just heard it once. Sing every verse of it. As far as singing is concerned, it was quite common to go to three millings a week. I was to four millings one week. And the homespun was five times as hard to mill as the blankets—the blankets were light, you know. They used to have some millings in the daytime and there'd be nobody there but women. And there were so many women then that could sing, beautiful singers and a lot of songs—no end. I remember millings right in this house—and the house was packed tight. They'd be in the kitchen—the harrow [milling board—*cliath*] would be right here. And people sitting around the room, and upstairs. And where the beams are cut there for the stairway, my father was quite nervous one night—there were so many up there in the hall there, that he was scared that the header would give way with the weight that went on it. But it didn't.

My father would be sitting there where the cat is there. He'd be so tired every night he'd be there— but if we'd start singing a song, part of one we'd heard at a milling—he'd

Three of the North Shore Gaelic Singers, left to right: John Alex John X. MacDonald, Thomas A. (Tommy Peggy) MacDonald, John Shaw (Seògan)

start over there and he'd finish it off—perhaps there'd be 13 or 14 verses. So there was no trouble to learn. He had them there in bushels. He learned songs though I don't think he ever composed any. But he told me one time there was a milling up at Donny's place and he was only 14—and boys of that age were to be home at 10 o'clock. Up till 18 or 19 you weren't out on the road, you were home. Really they were too young to go to the milling. They walked three miles. They went to the window to look in.

The window was up—the house so warm and a big fire on. And there was a fellow there singing a song that Murdoch MacDermid had composed from Wreck Cove. He made a song for a girl he had been going with and she had been in Boston and when she came back she had lost her Gaelic—it's in the songbook here—and my father outside the window. He had heard the tune but never heard the song. He told me himself that when he woke up in the morning, he was lying in bed, and he had the whole fourteen verses. Now I couldn't do anything like that. My father at 90, when he died—two weeks before he died, if you came to the house and asked him to sing a song he would, he'd remember it that well.

If there was anyone to sing the chorus, good and well; if not, he was going to sing it for you anyway.

I don't think they'd be singing anywhere else, only in the house. But I heard Malcolm Angus MacLeod talking about it up in Ontario. His father was a beautiful singer and his mother was still better. And they both had songs to no end. And he said there used to be this composer—this Norman MacDonald, he used to go to visit there—come in and have a smoke and then start singing songs. And it was quite common, he said, to sing for two hours, one after the other, one after the other. His mother would sing a song and his father would sing a song and this MacDonald fellow would sing. Most of the good singers learned the songs from end to end at home, from their parents. And that Norman MacDonald was pretty sharp, you know. If anything would happen, you know, he'd make a song. He made a song once about a milling frolic that was up the road somewhere, one fellow wanted to have a girl friend. Anyhow, I think what happened they all piled on the sleigh and when they were going down the road the sleigh broke and the horse ran away—and that was enough to start a song, you know. And he made another song, I don't know it, but I heard it sung, of fellows that used to trap out in the woods and they went out—R.J.'s father and another Urquhart, he was my uncle—and they were supposed to have got lost out in the fog and snowing and whatnot—and pretty hard up before they got back. They had some dogfish out there for bait. Dogfish, you know, it's not edible as far as we're concerned. But they used to take it ashore and split it up and dry it and take it out to the woods—use it for bait for lynx traps and the like of that. So the grub ran out on them and as a last resort they had to start eating the dogfish. And it was put together good. I know only three or four verses of it. How the events happened, how they got lost and all.

THOMAS A. (TOMMY PEGGY) MACDONALD: The custom was to have the cloth—the blankets and the homespun—soaked in warm water and oatmeal. I don't know why the oatmeal. Then when the crowd came, they'd bring it out—they wouldn't wring it out dry at all—just dry enough so it wouldn't drip on your knees. And then as the milling went on, after three or four songs, the water would be pretty well out of it. And they'd come around and sprinkle more water over it.

In some instances, like down at Wreck Cove where they had a regular milling board, with the big grooves, they used to have that and put it up in the different places where they'd have millings. But in most places all along here the people that were going to have a milling would always have lumber and make a milling board themselves. These would not have grooves. There weren't too many of the ones with grooves. They were just milling boards made on the same principle as the old-time homemade washboards, ridges in them. That was the idea of it. It would mill the cloth more uniform, better. If you have a bunch of smooth boards on the milling board, well, if they wouldn't be good old-time millers on it, they'd just swish the cloth along and it wouldn't have too much effect on it. The old-time millers, they'd usually start off by giving it a light pounding first, give it a hit and pass it, rub

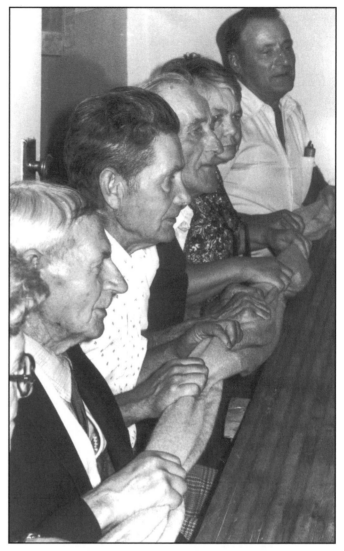

Sandy Kenny Morrison, Alexander Smith, John Shaw, Gwennie Pottie, Donnie Morrison

it along, passing it to the next fellow, he'd do the same—and that was bringing the nap out and shrinking it. And then when they'd come to the last part, the finishing it up, they'd just hold it in their hands and pound it on the table—not pass it along at all, just pound it—that really shrunk it, you know, that last going off. I think the idea of not giving it too much pounding in the start, it would shrink it too much in a hurry and not bring the nap out.

(*Who would make the decision to change from pound and pass to holding it in place and pounding it?*)

Well, the fellow who was leading the singing. When they'd get to that point, he'd hang on and then everybody would hang on to the cloth and pound and pound it instead of passing. No one would tell us. He'd just hold tight and that was the signal.

The table would be set up in the kitchen. The milling board was always put in the biggest room. And in some instances, I didn't see too many but it was quite common—when time came to have something to eat—usually the milling tables were pretty big because they'd all have a long piece of cloth probably—you'd have probably 10 or perhaps 12 on each side of the milling board—and the women would tell them to have a rest, we're going to eat. They'd take the whole thing to the milling board, take the cloth away, and they didn't have to move out of there. Very often they'd have baked beans, sometimes potatoes and meat, potatoes and fish—but very often a great big pot of nicely baked beans. Eat it right at the milling board. Biscuits and perhaps brown baked, Boston baked beans—brown bread. Then when they'd be through, another bunch would sit up to the milling board and have a feed.

Milling would start in some cases very early in the evening—and usually some of the women would have perhaps 30 yards of homespun. That is for trousers and jackets. And that required three or four, perhaps five hours of milling. And then perhaps 30 or 40 yards of blankets, which didn't require so much milling. In that case they'd very often have to start four or five o'clock in the evening in the fall of the year. Getting dark then, you know. And that would continue on till sometimes two and three o'clock in the morning. Because that old homespun, boy, required a lot of pounding and milling. Heavier stuff. When that was milled, it was that thick and stiff you could almost stand it up on the end. Great stuff. But the blankets, you know, I think the women watched that pretty closely so you wouldn't mill them too much—around an hour or a little better than an hour.

And millings were so common then. I remember the only time I was ever away from home working was in 1924—and I came home in November. And my mother had been weaving I guess most of the fall. I don't know just how much she had woven. And we were supposed to have a milling the following week. I came home on a Monday, and the following week there were three millings, and all in the same district. And the next week the same way, two or three millings. That went on till perhaps the latter part of December and it had started perhaps in October. Because everybody was weaving and they wanted to get the blankets milled. That was the pattern: probably every second household had their batch of cloth to be milled.

After you finish milling, there'd be two fellows get on one end of the milling board, two on the other end. The cloth was one long single strip, just as it came from the loom. If it had been sewn together at the end for passing around the table, it was taken apart for this. But very often where there was a great bunch of millers they didn't need to sew the ends together—they'd just watch for the end and pass it. Anyhow, they'd stretch the blanket out, and then just roll it up

Murdoch (the Chief) MacAskill, John Shaw, and Jessie Mary MacLeod

tight on the table—fellows on one end holding it back tight and the other two fellows rolling it up tight, right up to the finish. Then, when that was done, they turned it sideways, two strapping fellows now, one on each side of the board. Each gave the roll two or three whacks from the centre out. Then they unrolled it some—perhaps three or four feet—did the same thing—all the way till the end—just driving all the water out of it. And that finished it. After that they'd be washing it.

The same principle finished off the homespun. Roll it up right tight then start to unroll it. Two fellows, one on each side, banging it as they were unrolling it, and that would be it—two o'clock in the morning, sometimes quite a lot later than that. See, the women were pretty meticulous about that. It had to be shrunk to a certain width—I think it's 28 inches or 27 was it. And it was pretty hard to get to that

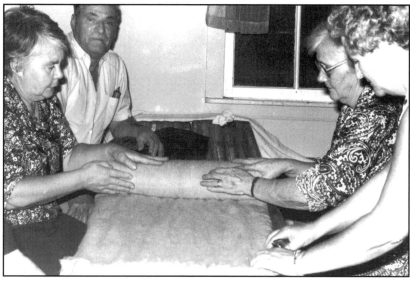

Rolling the milled cloth: Gwennie Pottie, Donnie Morrison, Evelyn Smith, Mary Morrison

last going off, because it was shrunk so much. But some of them insisted it had to be shrunk to that— keep singing, milling—three or four o'clock in the morning before they'd get it shrunk enough to satisfy. Kept measuring—a *cromadh*, they called it— that's the measure. That meant from the tip of

A traditional milling frolic meal served in the harrow: salt herring, blue potatoes, oatcakes, bannock, and good strong tea

A Milling Frolic on the North Shore

the finger to the knuckle. Most of them figured that, I think, as five inches. The one that owned the cloth would do that measuring—her finger. She had to be the boss to see that it was done to her satisfaction. Even if somebody else thought it was pretty good, if she didn't think so you'd have to go at it again. Three or four o'clock in the morning. And we wouldn't think anything of it then. And there was such a lot of them, you know. It would be hard work with that heavy homespun, swinging that around, perhaps a fellow would have a song with 25 or 30 verses in it—by the time that would be finished a fellow's tongue would be hanging out.

Weaver Gwennie Pottie with her finished cloth

(*You wouldn't think of not going?*) Oh, no. We'd go. It was great fun. (*And all you got out of it was a plate of beans?*) Plate of beans. Lots to eat, whatever they had—they always had lots to eat. If the milling was going on later than the usual hour, they would come around with tea perhaps one or two o'clock in the morning.

And you know, that song John Shaw sang the other night at the milling [at Josie Tommy MacDonald's, French River]—I haven't heard it since years and years till he sang it that night. That was the song they would sing when they were rolling the cloth. The singer started off, and he'd sing the chorus: *O co chuireas sinn anns an luing Eireannach?* Oh, who will we put in the Irish ship? Then if there were nine or ten around the milling board, you'd start at one end. Like if I was singing it and John Shaw was sitting there, I'd sing: It's John Shaw that we'll put in the Irish ship. [*Gur e John Shaw chuireas sinn anns an luing Eireannach.*] After that comes: *Cò fear tè óg a theid ri thaobh anns an luing Eireannach?* Who's the young girl that we'll put there with him on the ship? Then name one of the girls at the milling board, that she'd go with him. And it follows all around the milling board. One fellow would name the girl and the boy and all the rest would take in the chorus. We used to call them *"Oran Leannanachd"* [Courtship Song]. I remember when there were two or three of those kinds of songs. And some people would take offense if you'd name them and name a certain girl to go with them. Perhaps some fellow would do it for devilment. If there was a young fellow and his name was mentioned, then when it came to who were they going to put with him in the ship—perhaps they'd name an old crow of 70 or 80 years old. Used to get some of them wild.

In the barn

Wishie Rose at Sea

IT WAS SOME BAD WEATHER on that thing, but she was a good sea boat [the *Muddy*, his coastal boat]. We were out in Hurricane Hazel. We were taking up coal to the Madeleines [Magdalen Islands] a Friday, I guess. A fellow came down, said, "What about going to Caraquet for me—we got a truckload of fish boxes." I said, "We got 50 ton of coal in the boat yet." He said, "That's all right—good ballast. And the man who owns the coal, he's satisfied if you go, if you want to." He said, "A few dollars in it." I said, "That's all right. Tomorrow morning, we'll leave." So Saturday morning we left and went to Caraquet; we got over there Saturday night. Sunday afternoon we had everything aboard. We had 152 empty fish boxes, lengths of three-inch galvanized pipe on the back deck. We left. We got the forecast—they wanted sou'west 15 that night, sou'east 25 to 30 the next day, and then we'd be over on the Madeleines by that time, anyway. We left at four o'clock that Sunday evening.

About 10 o'clock I was in the bunk—by God, I heard the water going back over, you know—rain—spray water going back over the boat. I got out and the mate was at the wheel. I asked what was wrong. You couldn't see anything, the blinding rain then. He said, "Storm and wind." I said, "I know." I said, "Slow around a bit, it's only a bloody squall, probably only 15 or 20, something like that." He said, "It's a good 50 now, not 20." So we hove her in to for a while, slow, but it got worse. I said, "Swing her stern to it." We run it up nordeast, and when it start to come daylight, start hauling more to the west. Blow—God, didn't it blow. Like a fog, you know—wind.

Couldn't keep her broadside—too much sea, shallow water, too. So we got something to eat, we got a bit of breakfast. Just after breakfast—we had a life raft up on top, well-lashed to her—the sea struck her, and she parted lashings on the life raft. And it tore the insulator up through the set, the telephone, tore her up through the

Wishie Rose, Baddeck

roof of the house. Couldn't get ahold of anybody. I could hear Grindstone calling for a little while before the set got wet. I got the heel of a rubber boot, and I got out and drove it back, and got the wire down through, hooked on to the telephone again. By God, the red light came on. I called Grindstone—that was the middle of the day then. "Well," they said, "we've been calling you and calling you, where are you?" I said, "Well, we're out here somewhere."

I said, "What have you got for weather tonight in Grindstone?" He says, "We don't like to discourage you, we got 78 mile of wind." I said, "You're not discouraging anybody, old boy, we got just as much." He said, "Where are you?" I said, "I don't know." The sea used to break. If she'd strike her, you'd think she'd be like a matchbox. But the waves didn't hit her. They'd break before they'd get to her and they'd break after they'd pass her. We were just running slow with two engines, just to keep a serious way on her. I said, "I don't know—we should be 20 miles in back of the Madeleine Islands—we should be. But 'should be' and 'is,' I don't know." I said, "We're going down for Brion Island, somewhere down in that direction."

At two o'clock I said to the mate, "If you can get up on top of the house—if you can't, I'll try to get up—you might see some land. We got to be getting close in back of the Madeleines somewhere—I know we are." The sounder wouldn't sound; too much froth under the boat. I said, "If we don't see something pretty soon, I'm going to run her before us—we'll strike something before dark. It's easier to save your life in the daylight than it is in the dark."

Well, everybody was satisfied. He got up on top of the wheelhouse, and he wasn't up there long, tied onto the spar. "Skipper," he said, "I can see land—you might know where it was if you were up here." He got down and got in through the wheelhouse window. I got up, and the minute I saw it, I knew it—just exactly where we wanted to be—top of Brion Island—I knew it so well, I worked around there so much. I said, "You get to the wheel and open her wide open and get her going." I saw her scoop the water up over her head, trying to get through between Brion Island and the Bird Rock before dark. Only 10 fathom water at the most going through there, only 60 feet of water in that storm of wind.

Well, we went right through in the right place—it looked like she was breaking everywhere. But when we got through there, an hour from that we were up on the east point of the Madeleine Islands. We were all right. Twelve o'clock that night we were in Grindstone, tied onto the wharf. We had had 152 fish boxes on deck—you couldn't lash empty fish boxes—and we took off 150. We lost two overboard in that wind. That's how good she was.

Oh God, that boat was good. If you keep her clear of the rocks, she'd kill you before she'd drown you. She was that good. You won't believe this, but it's true. We had a little one of those ship-mate stoves in the fo'c's'le for cooking on, and it never was lashed. There were holes in the four legs of the stove on the block it was on, and there were just three-inch nails put down and bent over—that's all that was there—it never was lashed—and she never knocked a cover off all the time I had her. But you'd get her broadside on a roll, and she'd roll the milk out of your tea. But head on, you wouldn't know she'd ever blow. If she could steam, you could steam, she wouldn't hurt anything. She was a good old boat. They told me there at Grindstone, you couldn't see Entry Island all day for wind, and that's only 10 miles across to Entry Island from Grindstone.

In the early part of the century, the road was only a bridle path and Dingwall was inaccessible for weeks at a time during the winter. The first buggy track was cut out in 1925 and enlarged to a road over North Mountain and Big Intervale three years later. Still, it was not a comfortable journey and Anselme Boudreau remembers one trip on November 1, 1932, in which he left Chéticamp for Dingwall at nine o'clock in the morning, and reached his destination at eight o'clock that night. He was travelling by car. – from Judith V. Campbell's *Report of the Human History of Cape Breton Highlands National Park*

Moving the House off Fraser's Mountain

STARTING WITH THIS PHOTOGRAPH, I went to the Margarees. I knew that George MacDermid had taken the picture—Kenneth MacKenzie had told me that. For George, photography was more of a hobby. He never had a studio or made a business of it. I took the photo to Osgood MacPherson at his store in Margaree Valley. He knew the house and sent me to Vera Fraser. She knew some of the people, yes, she had lived in that house. The man to the right wearing the cap was her husband, Ernest. But the photo was before she came into the family. Vera sent me to Mary and William Crowdis. Mary is the little girl in front, to the left. She named everyone in the picture. Front row, from left: Mary Fraser Crowdis, Malcolm Fraser, Lillian Burton, John Burton. Back row, from left: Simon Fraser, Tena (Christena) Burton Fraser, Verne Burton, Florence Burton and Ernest Fraser. The

dog's name is Watch. The house is pictured where it now stands on the Egypt Road. It was moved there from atop Fraser's Mountain.

WILLIAM CROWDIS: Now lots of people think that they built it up, blocked it up, and dropped it. It came down just like this here. Let's say that my leg here was the mountain. They dug Samsons. [We've also heard it called "dead men."] They dug a hole in the ground, and they buried a Samson post there—a log that they could tie to, that would not give—and they put it on the upper end of the house—you know, that the house wouldn't tip over. It's very steep up there. They put the crop in or the hay—'twas in crop time because I was harrowing in the back field at our place. And I saw them coming down there, just coming in jerks, you know. It'd be holding and then let go and then come, but, this rope, this Samson—I believe the Samson went *through* the house and out through a window on the opposite side. And they put a stick across the windows for strength. Otherwise, you might pull the rear end off of it. I heard them talking that the rope went through the house and it went through a window to a stick on the opposite side. It kept it. 'Cause if it went end over end it would smash all to pieces.

This French fellow had the rigging—and that's the way it came down, just headfirst, like that. And to keep it from tumbling they had this Samson guide, and they had other equipment for pulling it, too. (*Did they jack it up and put skids underneath it?*) Oh yes. But then they pulled it off of the foundation and brought it down *with* the land. Now lots of people think they blocked it up and then dropped it down—but they didn't do it that way. It came headfirst. (*You mean the front of the house was facing down the hill, tilted down the hill?*) Yes. And he had a winch of some kind for pulling. Now, I wasn't there, but I heard the talk. They had winches for power to pull it down, and they had this rope fastened to this Samson that it wouldn't go end over end. It didn't break a pane of glass.

I don't think there was a horse at all that ever I heard tell of it. There were winches. It was done by men. You know, it was a dangerous place to put horses. Men could get out of the way if anything happened. But they said there wasn't a mishap in the whole thing—just as the man planned.

MARY CROWDIS: They split it. Took the main part first. Then took the kitchen down, William. It came down and he set it up down below there and they lived in the big part, and he went back up and he brought down the kitchen part and joined them together. **WILLIAM**: The Frenchman, he was the schemer. But there were a lot of people—they weren't like they have today—the people ganged right there to help them bring the house down. **MARY**: They didn't hire any-

body. **WILLIAM**: Hired nobody. Everybody went. The neighbours. This is a long time ago.

(*Do you remember when they moved the house?*) **MARY** : No, no, I was only six months old. (*Was there a community up there on Fraser's Mountain?*) No. There was just my grandfather went there in the wilderness—my grandfather, Malcolm Fraser. It was nothing but woods. And he cleared that Fraser's Mountain.

WILLIAM: I was reading this morning a history book that I have here. [From John F. Hart's *History of Northeast Margaree*: "Simon Fraser of Skye, Scotland, first lived in Prince Edward Island after coming to this side of the Atlantic. His wife was formerly Margaret MacDonald, sister of John MacDonald, who had settled at Rivulet, in Northeast Margaree. When Simon Fraser died in P.E.I., his widow moved to Margaree to be near her brother, bringing with her her three children, Alexander, Kitty, and Malcolm. Alexander went to the United States, Kitty married John MacLeod, and Malcolm settled on what is now known as Fraser's Mountain at Margaree Valley...."] Malcolm Fraser went up there and cleaned that out himself with oxen—you got underneath the root and pried it out—and burnt.

MARY: He just cleared the land like that, cleared that farm. **WILLIAM**: It's a big farm. **MARY**: There's nobody living there. **WILLIAM**: Now, he didn't do this in an evening. He was years doing this. (*And doing nothing else.*) Well, that was his idea of farming. **MARY**: That's what he had to do, making a living with that. **WILLIAM**: That's what everybody lived on.

MARY: He'd burn a piece of land and he'd plant his garden there—they called it the burnt patch. He planted turnips and potatoes. His family was all born there. My father, two of his brothers, and his two sisters—were all born up there. And they came down—my father took the house down. Where he took it there [on the Egypt Road], that was my mother's father's home—was the Burton property. But they *still* maintained the mountain farm. They made hay there. Now my nephew pastures his stock there. But right up until recently they made hay up there.

(*Is it because they came late they ended way up there on the mountain?*) Well, he couldn't have been very late, because he died way in his eighties and he was down there living with my father when he died—and he was only a young boy when he went up there and cleared that. He came with just his mother—his father was dead.

Well, if you'd see the farm you'd wonder how he ever did that. **WILLIAM**: And I've heard my father say, when the people down in Rossville here—and they were supposed to be big farms— were out of hay, they'd go up to Malcolm Fraser's on the mountain to get a little hay for to put in. Now this was very essential, for the horses to pull the plow, for to plant a few potatoes. They had no hay of their own, and that's where they'd go. He'd never take anything for it. He'd give them a cartbox full of hay. Which wouldn't be very much, but enough for to have to feed the horses for a day or night. He was that much advanced. It was good land up there.

MARY: It was so hard getting up and down the mountain, you know. But those old people, they never minded it. My grandfather used to come down to church two and three times on Sunday. Walk. **WILLIAM**: Well, twice. **MARY**: We were a Baptist, and they had service in the morning and at night, and if there was anything special going on, they would have it three times. Morning, afternoon, and evening. And he never missed. Walking, too. He wouldn't harness a horse to come down. He walked. (*Because it was Sunday?*) **WILLIAM**: No. If you had a horse, they did the work. That was what you had to plow or pull a root out or haul the stones away. **MARY**: The horse would rest on a Sunday afternoon.

(*Did you really get to know Malcolm Fraser?*) Indeed I did. I was quite a little chunk there [indicating the photo of the house that came off the mountain]. He was my favourite. There was never a man like him. As far as *I* know, as a child, he couldn't be any better. An A-1 man, that's all. He was a hardworking man— he was a very hardworking man—he was a religious man. And he was a good, good-living man—

that's all I can say. He was awful good to me. (*Where did he find time for you?*) Well, he was around 80 there. (*Wasn't working as much?*) No. He was lame. I don't know what ever happened to him that he was lame. He's buried up the Baptist church. The Baptist graveyard. **WILLIAM**: I don't believe there's a tombstone. **MARY**: Oh, I don't imagine.

MARY: Then after they moved down from Fraser's Mountain to where the house stands, after the Oxford Pulp and Paper Company started out St. Ann's—it was down on the North River [originally the North River Lumber Company]. You must have heard of it. But anyway, my mother cooked—my father and her went back up on the mountain and they worked for one of the superintendents, Charles Jackson. And they farmed that farm. And they had horses—oh, I suppose they'd have probably a hundred horses there at a time. **WILLIAM**: That is, the woods horses. They'd come out there when the haul was over. They came out and stayed the winter at the farm. That is, February and March and April. **MARY**: And my mother was a cook there. (*So this was the farm that served the Oxford Paper Company.*) **MARY**: That's right. They had it leased from my father. **WILLIAM**: They had it for perhaps 10, 15 years. And their crop was mostly potatoes for the woods. **MARY**: Potatoes and turnips. They raised a lot of vegetables. **WILLIAM**: Loads and loads and loads— they built a green cellar, too—a place for to keep them where they wouldn't freeze. **MARY**: And my mother and father went back up there to work when they opened that farm. The company built a little house up there—I suppose it's down now. And they had three big barns there. **WILLIAM**: Well, you think what it would take to keep a hundred horses. **MARY**: The old barn was still up there—but they had to do a lot of repairs to it. Then they built two other barns. Then they had a harness room and everything right there— had a man from Whycocomagh, he was a harness maker.

(*We've sort of lost that direct connection, between St. Ann's and Margaree, because we think*

of the road today, which is so long around. We forget that on top of the mountain, people weren't that far apart.) **MARY**: No, they used to go right in through St. Ann's and down to North River and Baddeck and those places. They had four horse teams.

(*And the road was pretty good then?*) **WILLIAM**: Well, put it the other way. They were pretty bad. They were mud and water and everything. I drove four-horse team there. Ernest Fraser did, too. And the lead horses, the ones that would be ahead, they'd be soaking wet with mud and water. You had to go in the barn and wash those horses down when you got into St. Ann's. **MARY**: Wintertime was the only time the road was really good. **WILLIAM**: But it was really a bad road. It wasn't a good road. Today they have a good road. When I started there first, we toted with two wheels and a drag. The front wheels—they were truck wagon. Then there were poles put on the bunk—and this is what they put the stuff on, on the rack. (*Poles right on the ground.*) Yes, "tail drag," they called it. (*And by "stuff"—what were you toting?*) Well, hay, oats, potatoes, flour, pork, every damn thing. **MARY**: Everything went in from this end. **WILLIAM**: There were barrels of lard and barrels of flour. Scarcity of nothing. Axes, iron, tools, saws, clothes—anything. This is what we toted in. Horseshoes, bolts and coal and everything for the blacksmith shops in there. And a sawmill in there, too. Used to make some of the stuff for making sleighs—big heavy sleighs—some were tail drag and some were two sleighs, you know, bobsleighs, they call them. And there were a lot of them tailing them, hauling pulp.

MARY: I stayed up on the mountain with my mother and father all the time she cooked. I stayed up there and went to school from there. I went to school down here in the valley—I walked up and down. They rented the farm and they kept horses there—well, they had to have a bunch of men there. And then there were men going back and forth to the woods from Chéticamp, even from the Madeleine Islands—from Mabou, Port Hood, all Inverness County—there'd be men working in St. Ann's. And she was cooking up there. And they used to stop and get their meals on the way in, 'cause they were nearly all walking. One day I remember of her, she gave 95 meals. (*This was a sort of halfway house then....*) Right. And she had a steady bunch at the mountain farm up there all the time.

WILLIAM: It was a kind of a bonanza for the people here. I used to butcher for them in there once. I was hired by another man, who was Malcolm MacLeod. He was in with this Jackson, and we used to go buying hay and go buying cattle. Oh, I've seen there where he lived—perhaps 50 to 100 head of cattle butchered—and they'd go in on the tote teams. So it was quite a thing for the country here to get rid of these. And they bought pork, too. And they bought potatoes sometimes, if they were short. Some of those camps had as high as 80 men, and there were a good many camps. It was a big industry, yes, for us anyway.

MARY: You know, a lot of their provision came by Margaree Harbour. **WILLIAM:** Even gasoline and kerosene. To Friar's Head. They hadn't too much of a capacity at Margaree Harbour for to land the stuff. And used to go to the Island and buy hay and oats and all. And sometimes it came in by rail, but if they could get it in by boat, it was much cheaper. Horses used to come in by rail, boxcars—brought in 30 or 40 horses at a time. And that wasn't all. They brought in by shipload to Murray [Road, St. Ann's Harbour].

You know, I worked in there for $1.35 a day. And today they're getting $60 to $70 a day. It makes me sweat. We cut pulp in there for a-dollar-something a cord, I think it was—and we paid a dollar for board. And we slept on boughs. You made poles, you know, and you put boughs across this way and fire a blanket over and that's the way you slept. Wasn't very comfortable. And

you had your shoes for a pillow, gumshoes. 'Twas pretty rugged. (*They didn't give you everything....*) Oh, far from anything.

And you know, I knew a fellow that worked in there, and he had a team of horses of his own in there. Getting along great. And he came out for Christmas. And his wife must have made a fire on or something. And he got a cold and he never got back that winter. The heat. He was so used to the cold. They just put moss in the cracks. But no one was sick in there. An odd one died in there, but very odd. Mostly the flu that got them in there. But that man—he came home for Christmas and he had to get somebody else to go back and get his team—he got such a cold when he got home that he couldn't go back. And he had never had a sneeze nor a snuffle nor nothing while he was in there. (*So as long as you treat them rough all the time, it's all right.*) Well, it seems like that.

Jack and Janie Nicholson, Baddeck

Dan E. MacQuarrie,
Middle River, in World War One

(*WHEN DID YOU GO to the military?*) 1907, I suppose. The militia. (*Why?*) Well, crazy to go to camp. Aldershot. Used to go up to Nova Scotia— Kentville, you know—camp out for two weeks. It was great. There was a company from Middle River—well, the companies were small, probably 50 men and officers. There was another company in Big Baddeck, Baddeck, Margaree, Inverness, and Iona. (*All separate companies in the militia?*) Yes. And they'd have the camp every year, around September. People would be through with their hay then. I went about six or seven years to that camp.

We'd drill at camp. Rifles. Uniforms. We had the red coats, same as the Mounties. We had tents. Go from here on the boat, the *Blue Hill*— and we'd get the train in Iona. Then we'd go to Truro and they'd shift up through the Valley. It was quite a trip for us young fellows. And everybody was crazy to go. They didn't have to coax them. Stay for two weeks. Drilling. Learn how to shoot. They had the old Ross rifles then. And when the war came, we took those Ross rifles overseas with us.

(*Was it more patriotic or fun?*) It was just fun. It got me in trouble, though. Well, I was called in in 1914. I was working in the lumber woods. And I got this letter to report next day in Baddeck. And we didn't know where we were going or anything else. We knew the war was coming.

And I did report—1914, August. And they sent us down to Marconi Towers—the wireless there—in Glace Bay. We were guards. They had about 50 masts there then, and they had—oh, it was foolish, when you come to think of it—had men hoisted up in them, up in the tower in a kind of a basket, watching, see if the enemy'd be coming. They kept men there all through the

war. Then there was a cable in Sydney Mines— had some men there. Had a cable in North Sydney. There was a cable up in Canso—had a company there. Those cables were going overseas. Vital to the country, you know, when the war was on. Whether they would be destroyed or not, I don't know.

We'd drill. And then we were on guard duty at night, so many. (*What did they tell you to watch for?*) Oh well, there were a lot of Germans and Austrians working in the mines here. They might come up there and blow it up. But there was no sabotage in Cape Breton in the First War.

I was away five years. Went a few months

to the towers there. Then I enlisted. We drilled a little while in Sydney, at Victoria Park. And then we went to Halifax and we were there for the winter—winter of '15. And the summer of '16 they sent us to Kentville. Then we went overseas from Halifax on the old *Olympic*. She was a big one—there were seven decks on her. Went from Halifax to Liverpool. We were on the ocean about five days, made it in five days. They had them stacked, boy, and it was wonderful the way they had it arranged. Every seventh man was appointed to feed, to draw the grub for six other men. There was no confusion. There were so many appointed every day. And we slept in hammocks. On deck. There were 7000 numbered—7000 men on that ship.

(*What did you think you were going to?*) We were going to our deaths, that's where we were going. Sixty thousand of them stayed over there, in the First War....

A bloody slaughter, that's what it was. And a lot of it was—they never should have sent them in to Passchendaele, because it wasn't fit for human beings. Just a mudhole. There were places there you could fall off the crack and be up to there. I saw fellows in to their hips, and it'd take three or four men to haul them out of it. It's hard to believe that, but it's true.

You saw death, mostly. Barbed wire. And mud. And probably fellows lying there, dead. I saw them when we'd be coming out, when we were in Passchendaele—and you'd see the stretcher-bearers coming out with the wounded fellows—and the wounded fellows were dead and the stretcher-bearers were dead, lying in the mud. We couldn't touch them. Somebody else would go in and do it.

Well, I can tell you right now, it was just the same as if it was a pure hell, that's what it was. I don't know how anybody ever came out of there alive. We had over 700 casualties there, in seven days. There were only about, probably a hundred, could answer roll call when we came out—killed, wounded, and missing. Of course, a lot of them were taken off to the hospital and we never saw them any more.

Oh my, we lost near all our officers there. I think there were only four officers left in the battalion. They weren't all killed, but wounded—and a lot of them were killed. Our colonel was killed there. Our second in command was killed there. And I don't know how many lieutenants—I just forget now. (*And common soldiers?*) Yes, lord.

I'll tell you how bad it was: They pulled us out, about probably 20 miles from Ypres. And we had to stay there for a whole month till we got reinforcements. There was nothing left. When I came out of there, the blood was running out of my feet. Blood, you know, and you couldn't have time to change your socks. She was rough.

(*What would they do with someone who died there?*) I'll tell you what they did with them—they were rolled up in a blanket and buried, with their shoes on. Be all they got. (*Cemetery?*) Oh yes, they had nice cemeteries—still there, and still looked after. Just two men that I saw put in a box. Two officers. The boys thought so much of them that they went to an old house and ripped the ceiling out and made a rough casket for them. No, none came home. The Americans sent their dead home.

(*Where were you when the war ended?*) We were in a place called Bethune. A little town. There's where we were when we got the word that she was gone, ended. (*Were you fighting the day before?*) Yeah, and there were 11 of our boys killed that day. And that was the sad part of it. One day, and they'd be safe. (*How were you told?*) The officers got the message. They signed in an old railway car. You might have heard that. It came over the wire; they had telephones, you know. Told us the war was over.

And of course, the Germans were pulling out, for home. We started following them. Followed them right into Germany, across the Rhine Bridge.

Oh Jesus, their horses were dying everyplace. When we were on the way to Germany, they were trying to pull some of their guns back, and you could see where the horses would give up, dead alongside the road. The guns were still there. And I saw a couple times there was a big piece cut out of the rump of the horse—they must have been getting hungry. I guess we took about two weeks following them. Till we got to Germany. And they didn't keep us there, though. None of us were allowed into Berlin. It was out of bounds.

(*What did you do to celebrate?*) Came back, and this is where we found the wine cellar—in a castle in Belgium. And we stayed there over six months. (*Drinking?*) Yes, there was quite a bit of drinking. I know, myself and another fellow from Glace Bay, we were pals. He died last fall. And I went to bed—you just think of the luxury of getting into clean sheets, a good mattress, after sleeping on the ground. We were put there, you see, there was room for so many men there; I forget how many. It was a big castle. But every man had a bed.

My friend came up and he shook me by the shoulder. He said, "Get up!" He was drunk, you know. "What the hell is going on?" I said. He said, "We found a wine cellar."

Well of course, I got up too, and went down; and we started helping ourselves to the wine. It was in shelves there, in the basement. It was fellows from Glace Bay found it, too. Started exploring, you know, and they saw this door, and wondered what was behind the door. Well, the door didn't last long with those fellows, it was broken in. Here was this big wine cellar, and quite a bit of brandy there, too. They called it cognac over there.

Well, we started lugging it out—we got feed bags—and hiding it. We were putting it into the hedges. And the room I was in, there was a flue going through it. There was no fire in it, of course. We started shoving it up the flue as far as we could reach. We had it there for months. They never bothered us.

Oh, they found out, all right; a lot of them were drunk the next day. The colonel raised hell, said, "You fellows will have to pay for that." And they boarded the door up. They put a guard on

the door. Had a guard on it day and night. And this fellow was on, I guess, in the evening. A person waited for him to leave for a little while, the devils, and they broke in again. And I guess they practically cleaned her the second time. Well, anyway, Colonel Ralston said, "We'll have to pay for it." But he went to see the fellow that owned it, or got into communication with him, and he said, "No. Give it to the boys. Only for them, I wouldn't have a castle left." He was a rich Belgian. I don't know what business he was in, but he must have been damn rich, because it was beautiful. There were glass doors and everything in that place.

(*When did you come back to Canada then?*) We landed back, I think, the 13th of June, 1919. We landed in Québec, the bunch I came with. We came up on the *Empress of Berlin* to Québec, and we came down to Halifax by special train. We got our discharges there. We were only in Québec one day. We had a parade through the town—you know the hilly city it is, cliffs up and the houses on top. And of course, we paraded to the train. And a special train came down to Halifax.

(*How were you greeted in Halifax?*) Well, I'd say it was rotten. We couldn't get a drink there—Prohibition was on, you see. The only way you could get a drink there was to go to the vendor. Had all the saloons closed down. Some of the fellows said, "To hell with it—let's go back to Britain!" Well, I went to a house, a fellow I knew, he was a MacDonald. And we used to visit him—he was a Cape Bretoner—and I told him my story, that I couldn't get a bottle of beer. He said, "I'll get you a beer. I'll get you a whiskey, too," he said.

(*How'd you get home to Middle River?*) Came down by train. And when I got into Baddeck, do you know how many cars were in Baddeck? Landed at Iona and got over on the boat. The *Blue Hill* was running then, twice a day; it met every train. And there were just two cars in Baddeck, and I came home in one of them.

And I went to work in a few days, haymaking.

Johnny Murphy Remembers Hilda

IT TOOK WHAT LITTLE I HAD to marry Hilda and buy this place. We had 14 children. One child—I gave the doctor two barrels of carrots and a ton of hay to pay him. Imagine. I never had any trouble making a living as far as eats, such as it was. It was these doctor bills and taxes—that was the two headaches. There were six of mine operated on for appendix.

For a living, I did everything. Played for dances, lumbered, farmed. One summer I got up at half past three in the morning and I milked six cows, loaded a load of manure and went into the Normaway and spread it before seven o'clock and got two dollars and a half for the load of manure. Then I hooked into the walking plow and I plowed 18 days there—10 hours a day. I got $5.85 for the 10 hours. One summer I got 50 cords of pit props for the old country, England. Six feet long. Draw shaved. And at the side of the road we got six dollars a cord. And they couldn't be over six inches at the top nor couldn't be under three inches. Now can you imagine? I got 53,000 feet of boards for the Forum in Sydney—and put over the rail onto a boat at Nyanza I got $14 a thousand. I paid $75 for that strip of lumber. I cut it and hauled it, put it over the mountain into a pile—2,100 logs. Sawed it. Loaded it on a truck, hauled it to Nyanza and put it on a boat for $14 a thousand.

Of course, for food we used to buy different then than we do now. For winter, get in 10 to 12 barrels of flour, get 10 or 12 gallons of kerosene for the light—and one year I got 1300 pounds of sugar. And as far as cheaper, I know for one hundred pounds of sugar I hauled logs two days with a team of horses to pay for it—around seven dollars a hundredweight. Thirteen hundred pounds of sugar sounds like a lot—but when you go feeding 45 meals in a day. And tomorrow the same thing. You can figure there was 14 of us. Three fourteens is nearly 45—and there'd be extra meals even if nobody came—children have to eat before they go to bed. You can figure Hilda was getting at least 45 meals a day. A 200-pound barrel of flour—she cooked that in a month. She was slaving.

And can you imagine carrying the water for to wash for those children? Christ, makes a lump in my throat when I think of what she had to do. And the money that they're throwing around now. People are spoiled today. It's outrageous when you think back—no lights, no hot water, carried water and heat it on the stove—that's hellish. She worked like a slave. She'd do the laundry and ironing at night—you imagine

Johnny Murphy Remembers Hilda

washing for all those kids just on a scrub board. I don't know how she did it.

Hilda and I would play together. When the kids were small Mrs. Connors would come down and she'd look after the kids for us, poor old thing—and stay till two o'clock in the morning. We'd play for showers and weddings—and I'll tell you. I never want to take money for showers or weddings—I never would do that. But then we played for school dances and people would dance. That was an awful job. No pick-up or anything. You'd be played out, press so hard on the bow so they could hear it. We'd get paid 10 or 12 dollars for a night.

Compared to Hilda's, my work was just ordinary work, you know. You just went out and worked. But hers was *care*. My God, look here, you take the care of those kids, up at night. There was one, the little girl that died—she was 16 months old—I am sure Hilda didn't sleep two hours in six weeks, up with that child. She was sick for six weeks. And she never smiled nor never cried from the time she took sick. I was never any good in the house. Like I told her when we first got married—she wanted to learn to milk—your work is in the house and my work is

outside and you're not doing anything outside because if you start doing anything outside, then I'll be expecting it.

Hilda was very religious. She'd walk to church and take those kids by the hand in deep snow and, look, stay up all hours of the night to teach them their catechism—nobody knows. Somebody'd come in and perhaps stay till 10 or 11 o'clock. I'd go to bed. I'd say, "Hilda, get in bed." "Go to sleep," she'd say, "I've got my prayers to say." She'd pray for hours. I'll bet she'd stay up till two o'clock some nights praying. And she'd light those candles. And if we were going anywheres for a drive and she forgot her beads— if I was halfway to the Forks I'd have to go back and get them.

She did the praying and I did the cursing— that's awful but it's the truth. I wish she was still living today, when we could enjoy—that we could go driving, you know. She worked too hard. She would not stop. She wouldn't stop. We had 14 children. There's 12 living. And there's 54 grandchildren. And I think it's 14 great-grandchildren. She never growled nor ever complained. You imagine. I'm not bragging, but by God, she was a great woman.

Hilda chords while Johnny fiddles, Margaree

Gluskap's Journey
—a Mi'kmaw Geography
of St. Ann's Bay and Beyond

IN 1915 F. G. SPECK took down a number of Cape Breton Mi'kmaq tales from the dictation of Chief Joe Julian of the Sydney band, and John Joe of Whycocomagh. They told him of the wonderful being, Gluskap. They told him:

One time when Gluskap had become the Indians' God, Christ wanted to try him to see if he was fit: so he took Gluskap to the ocean, and told him to close his eyes. Then Christ moved close to the shore an island which lay far out to sea. When Gluskap opened his eyes, he saw it. Christ asked him if he could do as much as that. Then Gluskap told Christ to close his eyes a while. When Christ opened his eyes, he found that Gluskap had moved it back to its place again.

Gluskap's Journey

Gluskap was the god of the Mi'kmaq. The great deity Ktcni'sxam made him out of earth and then breathed on him, and he was made. This was at Cape North, Cape Breton—on the eastern side. Gluskap's home was at Fairy Holes. Just in front of the caves at this headland are three little islands in a straight line, long and narrow, known as Ciboux Islands [today's Bird Islands]. These are the remains of Gluskap's canoe, where he left it when it was broken. At Plaster Cove (Two'butc, "Looking Out") two girls saw his canoe broken into three pieces; and they laughed, making fun of Gluskap. At this he told them that they would forever remain where they are; and today there are two rocks at Plaster Cove which are the remains of these girls.

Next, a little farther north at Wreck Cove, Gluskap jumped from his canoe when it foun-

dered, lifting his moose-skin canoe-mat out, and left it on the shore to dry. It is there today. There is still to be seen a space of 15 acres of bare ground where the mat lay. Then he started on and went to Table Head (Padalodi'tck) on the south side of Great Bras d'Or. Here he had his dinner. Next he struck into Bras d'Or Lake straight to Whycocomagh, on the western end, where, at Indian Island (Wi'sik, "Cabin"), he started a beaver and drove him out, following Bras d'Or Lake to St. Patrick's Bay. At Middle River he killed a young beaver, whose bones are still to be seen there.

Then Gluskap followed the big beaver until he lost track of him for a while. He stood at Indian Island and took a piece of rock and threw toward the place where he thought the beaver was. This rock is now Red Island. This started the beaver up and he ran back through St. Peter's Channel and burrowed through underneath, which is the cause of the crooks and windings there now. Then the chase continued outside in the ocean, when the beaver struck out for the Bay of Fundy. Here at Pli'gank ("Split Place"), Split Point, Gluskap dug out a channel with his paddle, forming Minas Basin, Nova Scotia. There he killed the beaver. Near here is a small island, which is the pot in which he cooked the beaver; and there, too, is another rock near Pot Rock, which is Gluskap's dog, left behind at this time. Turtle (Mi'ktcik) was Gluskap's uncle. Here with his pot and dog he turned Turtle into a rock and left them all there. Near where he killed the beaver are still to be seen the bones turned to rock. When he broke the channel to Minas Basin to drain the water out, in order to uncover the beaver, he left it so that today the

Gluskap's Journey

water all drains out at each tide. So Gluskap caused the Bay of Fundy tides. Then he crossed over eastward and came out at Pictou, where there were many Indians living. While there, he taught the Mi'kmaq how to make all their implements for hunting and fishing—bows, arrows, canoes and the like.

After a while he prepared to leave, and told the Indians, "I am going to leave you. I am going to a place where I can never be reached by a white man." Then he prophesied the coming of the Europeans and the baptism of the Mi'kmaq. Then he called his grandmother from Pictou, and a young man for his nephew, and departed, going to the other side of the North Pole with them. Again he said, "From now on, if there should ever be a war between you and other people, I shall be back to help you."

He is there now, busy making bows, arrows and weapons for the day when the white man may bother the Mi'kmaq. The Mi'kmaq are Gluskap's children. As he prophesied it came true, for in 1610 the first Mi'kmaq were baptized and became Christians. Gluskap had de-

parted just a little before them, because he knew he had to make room for Christ; but he is the Mi'kmaq's god and will come to help them if they ever need him. When Peary discovered the North Pole, he saw Gluskap sitting on top of the Pole, and spoke to him.

"Gluskap's Journey" includes mention of Fairy Holes, caves well-known by fishermen in St. Ann's Bay. Mr. Speck wrote that about 1860 "five Indians—Joe Bernard, Francis Bernard, Clement Bernard, Joe Newell and Tom Newell—entered the caves which honeycomb this headland, carrying seven torches. They walked as far as the torches would light them, about a mile and a half, found eight brooks in the caves, and when they came out discovered how a rock 300 feet wide had moved since they had entered. The Indians regard these caves as very mysterious."

Tommy Peggy MacDonald of the North Shore reported in the 1970s that people used to tell of a dog that went in the Fairy Holes and came out some days later at Ross Ferry—and when he came out the hair was all off him. Others told the story, and although he was said to come out different places it was always without any hair.

Claire, Julie, and Marie

Danny Mike Chiasson, Belle Côte

MY FATHER WAS A STONE-MASON. And had a little farm. And he was almost the only veterinarian that there was in this part of the country. And he travelled from Chéticamp to Margaree Forks.

(*Was he a professional veterinarian?*) No, no. But he had worked in the mines, in the stables there. And he used to work a lot with a veterinarian there. In Glace Bay. And he learned a lot from that. And when he came back to the country, there was no veterinarian. It's only in the last few years that there is such a thing in this part of the country. I don't know if there is any now, because there's no more cattle or anything left. But there was for a few years.

So. He used to travel from Cap Rouge to Margaree Forks. He spent most of his days—though he should have been home. He'd do that, and he had nothing for it. And the farm would go back here. He spent too much time on the road. You know, in those days, he didn't dare charge anything. He had no license, number one. And he was good-hearted, number two. So he spent a lot of the time when he should have been home.

Although he made a good living—it was a good living. He was a stonemason or farmer—that was his trade. But being a veterinarian would be in the evening. Spend half of his nights on the road.

So, when he died, they thought that I should do the same. You know, that I should do the doctoring. So I did, for a few years. Wasn't a qualified vet, but I had learned from him. And I read, you

know, I had a fairly good education—Grade 12. But he couldn't write his name when he first started out. But my mother taught him enough so that he could write his name on a cheque or a bill or the like of that.... He learned more after he got married. But you couldn't fool him on figures....

(*As a veterinarian, what would you do?*) Well, I'd try and find out how the animal acted, and try and make up my mind what was wrong with her. And then, I read. After being around with my father, and reading, I got so I could doctor an animal. To a certain extent. I wasn't a veterinarian, but in lots of cases I would have success—probably the same my father did.

(*Did you have medicines?*) Oh, yes. Well, it was all prepared—stuff that you'd get from Raleigh or from different companies. It was pretty well written on the directions what it was good for and how to administer it. (*Did you take anything from the woods?*) No. In my days I didn't use that. We always bought the prepared medicine when I did some veterinary work.

(*And did you have to come when cows were going to give birth?*) Oh yes, I think that was probably the first start I had, was in that. Because my father had been in that, and they thought I should be able to do it too. (*What were some of the things you had to do?*) Ha! Get the calf out! Some way or other. And sometimes, you know, with some help, and dislodging the calf, they'd get the calf out. Which probably on their own would never.

(*And did you perform operations?*) Oh, yeah. Probably more than I should have. Probably if the right party had got me, I'd have been hung. I bled horses—take about probably a quart of blood out. (*What was that good for?*) Well, if the animal was rundown, apparently the blood—I saw my father doing that. He would take a quart or more of blood out of an animal. And in 10 minutes after, you'd put it on your hand and just in one—it was just in a lump. And you'd throw it out, and there were no more signs of blood on your hand than there is today.

(*I don't understand that.*) Leave it—you know, just while they were talking—leave it in the bucket. After a while you could pick that up. It would kind of gel. And you'd take it up in your hand, and you'd throw it out. And there wasn't any more sign of blood on my hand than there is today. (*And was that a sign that the animal was sick?*) Well, it was a sign that there wasn't much good red cells, you know, when you wouldn't even have the colour of blood on your hand. That's what I made out.

(*So by bleeding the animal, how long would it take that animal to perk up?*) Oh, I've seen some of them in three weeks, a month—you'd never know the same animal. Of course, they wouldn't work for that length of time. But in three weeks time, I've seen some animals—the same animal—if you had a picture in both cases, you wouldn't know that it's the same animal in this world. (*The bleeding helped them that much.*) Oh, well, yes.

(*And where would you take the blood from?*) From the vein here, in the neck. And there's a set of fleems here in the house. Fleem—what they call fleems—to bleed. It's a rig—it's like a knife with a little blade attached to it. And that was sharp as anything. And you'd put a string on their neck to bring out the vein, and you'd tap that with this, and the blood would come out. You'd get a, oh, gallon or so of blood. It was good, also, for blood poisoning. I've seen horses—driving a nail in their hoof, and got blood poisoning from it. (*So you would draw some blood then.*) Draw some blood.

If a veterinarian'd hear me today, he'd say I'm crazy, but there's no matter. (*But you don't think you're crazy.*) Well now, I'm not sure yet! (*And you think it worked.*) Yes, yes, it worked.

Those days, people fed a lot of turnips to animals—cows. Now, the worst thing you could do was to cut a turnip. Most times they cut a turnip, or even a big beet—they wouldn't cut it right. Cut it all in kind of triangle shapes. And they'd go to swallow—you know, a cow has only one set of teeth. They wouldn't chew it, they'd swallow it. And the first thing, they'd have one of those in their throat. We fed hundreds of barrels of turnips, for a number of years, and we never cut one. (*Ah—gave it to them round.*) Round. And they'd start—you know, just scraping it, like. You know, we started with big turnips, to make sure they couldn't start to swallow it. And we fed—I remember having a hundred barrels of turnips here in the fall, and fed every one that way.

But, every other day—my father before me, and I after that—you'd get a call to go and see an animal that had a piece of turnip or a big potato in their throat. Well, I had a hose—two and a half, three feet. And I had a piece of wood to make kind of a handle with. And then, you have to get that out. If it was a big piece that you got inside of their mouth, you probably could sometimes get it out. But, usually you had to push it down. There's a hose around here yet, somewheres around the place, that I had for that. Many's the one I pushed down....

And then, there was another thing that used to cause some trouble was a warbler fly. It's a fly inserts something in the skin, and then you get a boil. A boil like. After a while, when it's ready, you can squeeze it like a—like a worm, you'd squeeze it, when it was right, and then it could come up. When it was ripe. But if you didn't—if you happened now—I've seen it sometimes right under the saddle, you know. And if that would squeeze in there, then you were in trouble. It would start festering, and then you had a mess....

(*Now, in the Scottish parts of the island, they often talk about the evil eye.*) Oh, yeah. (*Did they have that here?*) It was talked about, but there was nothing to it. That was just like if I wish you were somewheres else today instead of in here. You might have something going wrong with you. But that was all there was to it. You might as well wish for the sun. There was a lot of sicknesses caused by ill feed or wrongdoing of a man, that would cause an animal to act—and they blame it on the evil eye. To me it was all negligence or ill feed or something. As far as the evil eye, that's out. It's just like believing in ghosts. Just about the same. Evil eye and the ghosts, to me, are about the same. (*There's no truth at all....*) No. As far as I'm concerned. Because, I've been bad enough, if there were any ghosts, the devil would come around me—I'd have seen him around!

(*Because, I've talked to people who would have an animal, or horse maybe, down, lying on its side. And they'd go and they'd get some water from a brook into a pan. And they'd put a coin in that pan, I think a silver coin. And there was a prayer that they'd say over it. And then they'd throw this water on—right down the length of the horse. And very soon after, the horse would get up and be feeling better.*) Ha. And did you believe the story? (*Well, I don't judge them that way.*) A person that would believe that would believe in ghosts.

(*Do you think prayer can help a horse?*) Well, it would—I'd say—yes, prayer can help a horse, and help you, and me. I think if we prayed more, probably we'd get along better. I believe that there's a fellow up there, the Almighty is there. I think so.... I believe in prayer. But I think

you've got to do your share, you've got to carry a part of the load....

(*Did they do anything to help chickens?*) Not very much. We never had enough or never interested enough—no, not too much on chickens.

Pig was about the same. Pigs were a hard animal to doctor. It was hard to keep it still—unless it was stretched out so sick that you couldn't do anything with it. And the scream of it would scare the devil. So you didn't—there wasn't too much. They used to have some commercially prepared stuff that you'd just put it in their feed. And then, if they were constipated, bound up—an injection of hot water and soap through the rear end. It would help—I used that in any animal for that.

(*What else did you do for a living?*) Stonemason. I was going for anything. I was a schoolteacher for a number of years. And that I didn't like. I wasn't made to be cooped into a building. I had to be out in the open....

(*I understand that you were an artificial inseminator.*) Yeah. (*What does that mean?*) That means breeding a cow. The station where they had the bull was in Truro. And they'd mail it to me. And then I'd use it. It was in a little vial, and packed in ice. And, it's taken [from the bull] today, and tomorrow I'd get it. And that evening—I always tried to use it the same day if possible. I'd sooner go out at night and give the cow with the semen that was fresh, than to wait for the next day. You know. It's not going to last too long. The semen will eventually be of no more value.

(*Would you have trouble giving that to the cow?*) No. (*And did you do that a lot?*) Well, I don't say a lot. Not like in big places, but probably 15 or 20 a day, between here and Chéticamp, Margaree Forks. That's at the most, you know. But, lots of times there's only three or four, or two or three. I travelled from Margaree Forks to Petit Étang.

(*Did farmers prefer that to having the...?*) The bull. Oh yes, it was less trouble. You know, depending again on the farmer and a lot of things. It wasn't quite as sure as the bull. But, again, probably they weren't careful enough themselves, you know, and didn't call in time, or called too early, or the like of that. But I always had pretty good results. I don't believe it was much under 80%. That was almost as good as the natural breeding process.

I would get the semen in the mail every night. Every day you'd get that package. All year round. Year round. (*You must have bred a lot of cattle.*) Well, there wasn't that many. About—oh, God— less than a thousand a year. And that was from Northeast Margaree to Cap Rouge, almost.

(*And did you ever really retire as a veterinarian, or as a breeder?*) Yes, yes. Then there's another fellow took it over. But he was only at it a year or so when people quit keeping animals. Today, there's very few animals being kept. You wouldn't find—not half a dozen cows from here to Chéticamp. At one time every place had a cow, or two or three or four or five. In those days a cow meant a lot to a family, you know.

In olden days there was no such a thing [as an artificial inseminator]. I was probably the first that started here, when they started. Before that, everybody, or every other fellow, had a bull. And it got so that they weren't allowed anymore to keep them. They were on the road, getting in trouble. So, there was one time there that cows were nonexistent in this place, until artificial breeders came for a few years. And it's almost going back to the same thing again today, that there's none.

And if a car struck an animal on the road, you were liable for it. The owner of the cow. No matter what was wrong with the driver. Your animal wasn't supposed to be on the road.

They'd roam. Or sometimes they'd jump. You know, some of them could jump over half the height of this building. Or tear a fence down and get out on the road. And if a car struck it— even if you did it intentionally—the cow was to blame. You'd get soaked for it. You paid the expenses, you paid darn dear. Some of them played the game and got a lot of money. And many's the one that rid of their cow on that account. (*And I guess the bulls would be more likely to get out than the cows.*) Oh, yes, yeah. (*So they got rid of the bulls first.*) Yeah. In lots of districts they had what they called a "society bull." The bull would do probably from halfway between here and Margaree Church, and as far down again. They had a bull—fellow kept it. And you'd have to take the cows there to breed them. They were penned in—weren't allowed to roam.

(*But then they got rid of the society bull?*) Yeah, then. (*And then you became the breeder.*) Yeah. When they had a cow that had to be bred, they'd call me. So I'd wait—well, probably the forenoon or almost the forenoon. Then I'd start out, and go call. (*Did you say full moon or forenoon?*) Forenoon. (*Would the moon have anything to do with it?*) No. Don't believe in those things. (*You would if it worked.*) Yeah, but it didn't work.

At first, Swedish miners came from northern Ontario for the dynamiting. Then, according to Jim Daley: "I worked on the Trail right up there to MacKenzie Mountain. That was hard up there. You have French Mountain first and then a stretch on top and then MacKenzie. It was unbelievable, the blasting and jackhammering, the work that was done there. It was mostly built by people around here, around the Trail in different communities. They brought in some key men, engineers and that, but as far as 90% of the work, it was local people who built it."
– from Judith V. Campbell's Report

John J. and Sadie Theriault

JOHN J. THERIAULT, *Smelt Brook*: I was born in South Harbour about four miles from here. I never went very far. The wife was born in South Harbour, too. We had eight in the family—two boys and six girls. We lost—one of our boys was killed.

(*What were you raised to be?*) I was raised to be a poor man! And I'm still poor....

I used to leave home here—Sadie knows—you contradict me if I'm not right, please. I used to leave home in the morning and travel to North River woods [lumber camps]—it's over a hundred miles . And we wouldn't quite make it that night. We'd stay at the Halfway House. Do you remember anything about the Halfway House? (*I do know that it existed.*) It was about half between here and North River.... All the people that were travelling would stay there overnight.

(*And you would walk up from Smelt Brook to North River?*) Walk up! Walk up and walk

back. Well now, to finish it right. We'd go to North River, we'd work maybe a month. I had to leave home, and leave my wife with little children to look after while I was there. She had to get wood and saw wood and keep the house going till I got back. Joe Asseff, a merchant at White Point, he was our dealer. So, I'd go to Joe Asseff and I'd get stuff enough to do me for two or three weeks, you know, to come back. And when I came back, then, what money I had made at North River, I took it down and paid him off for his bills. I always was a pretty honest man. Everybody'll tell you that, that knows me. We paid our bills off.

And then, the next month, we're short of stuff again. No money. So, back to North River again. Isn't that right?

SADIE THERIAULT: Yeah. And then he ran the mail for 15 years from Smelt Brook here to White Point, from White Point to Neil's Harbour.

By foot…. He'd take the mail there, on his back. And there was no road. He had to open a path through the alders, to go through it. And maybe some nights it'd be 12 o'clock when he'd get home. With the mail. He'd have a bag of mail, big bag of mail strapped on his—in the summertime, now—strapped onto his back, and another one in front. Especially catalogues. When those catalogues would come out.

JOHN: Three times a week it was. (*And was there a lot of mail in those days?*) Oh, sometimes it was all I could manage. Sometimes all I could carry back. Of course you could carry 50 or 60 or 70 pounds, you know. But that's a heavy mail on your back. At that distance. There was four miles through the woods to White Point. It was two miles from White Point up to here. That was six miles. It'd be 12 miles two ways. I had to go and come. That was 12 miles a day. (*Three times a week.*) Three times a week.

(*And what did they pay you to do that?*) [John J. laughs.] I hate to tell you. I got $15 a month for two months, and every three months I got $17.50. It wasn't very much. Sometimes I used to have to get somebody to run the mail for me, see. Maybe it was better for me. And I'd go to North River to try to make some more money. Wasn't making enough to live on.

(*Was this all year round that you took the mail, or only in the fine weather?*) No, all the year round, winter and summer. Sometimes I used snowshoes in the winter. I used to make the snowshoes myself…. **SADIE**: Snowshoes and hand sleigh in the wintertime.

(*And it would rain sometimes?*) **JOHN** [laughing]: Oh, yes. It wasn't too bad, you know, but I got wet different times. I can't remember just how often. But when it rained I likely got wet. Sometimes I had oilcloths. You can't walk a distance like that with oilcloths on very good. It's almost better to be wet. In the summertime.

SADIE: Well now, a real stormy day, he wouldn't go. **JOHN**: If it wasn't fit to travel, I wouldn't have to go. If it wasn't fit to travel….

I've been caught in many, you couldn't see a hand before—you'd put snowshoes on, of course, you know. When you're used to that, you don't mind it so much. **SADIE**: But there'd be always two men go out. If there was a storm, there'd be always two men go meet him.

JOHN: When you're born in a place like this, you don't take much notice of bad weather. You know that. You know, you're used to it. Now a stormy day didn't mean a thing to me. I couldn't see a hand before, I'd get out cutting wood or hauling wood just the same as if it was fine. And you rigged up for it, too, see.

SADIE: We had two cows and a pig and hens. Oh yeah, we had a nice farm here. (*And of course, when he was away….*) I had to do it. (*And you did it all?*) Oh, yes. When milking time came, I had to lug the baby. I used to take the baby and lay her on a blanket inside the fence. I'd milk the two cows, and then I'd lay the milk out, bring the baby home in the house, and go back and pick the milk up. That's the way I got along when he was away.

(*And did you have lots of small children at the time?*) Oh, just about a year between them all. The last three there were about two years between them, but the first ones were just about a year between them. Always had a baby.

JOHN: The only stories she can give you is hard work. She always worked hard. Still working hard, knitting—knitting socks and mats, hooking mats. Yes, that's what she's up to. Two hundred dollars' worth—hook now, and she can sell them in the summertime. She never stops.

SADIE: Yeah, he carried the mail for 15 years on his back to Neil's Harbour.

JOHN: Snowshoes, and skis, and skates. I used skates on the crust—skated back and forth over the mountain, where they're coming with the road now. And take my skates off and go into the post office and get the mail, and put it on my back, and come back. Tie my skates on and skate back to where I put them on, going. Harden some more by the next day.

And skis, sometimes skis, I'd use skis on my feet. Every way that I could make it easy for me….

SADIE: Oh, my dear—we [girls at home] did everything. We had to do everything. We planted potatoes in the spring, and then we moved to the Point [White Point], where my father—to go lobster fishing. We stayed down there till the first of September. We worked in the factory, me and my two sisters—lobster factory. And then we'd leave White Point the last of September and come back up home [to South Harbour]. And dig the potatoes, and put the potatoes away. Then you'd have to start getting the hay for the winter.

My father—they fished till November, him and my brother. And then they'd quit fishing and come home. Then the winter's work started. Hauling hay, putting that away in the barn. Everything was done before the snow ever came. We didn't have any hay, see. The farm—the place we had wasn't big enough for hay. And we had a horse and two cows and some sheep. So he used to buy his hay.

So as soon as he came home and got settled down from fishing in November, he started hauling his hay. Got it all put away for the winter. Hay first, see. And then started cutting wood—sawing it and splitting it and piling it.

(*So you had a home at South Harbour.*) We had a home at White Point, too—a summer home. Just while they were lobster fishing.

The whole family'd move down the last of May. Father'd go down and set his traps, him and my brother. And then the last of May, by that time we'd have all the potatoes in, see, and everything done home, in South Harbour. And then he'd move us down—the whole family. We'd stay at White Point till the last of September. Then it was time to move back home to South Harbour, to dig the potatoes and get things fixed up for the fall. Then he'd stay down there codfishing, him and my brother, till November. Then he'd move home, too.

(*And when you'd go down there—did the whole family move—all 16 of you?*) The whole family moved—the whole family moved to White Point, for just the fishing—lobster fishing. We'd go down the last of May and we'd move back the last of September. (*That's a big family to take….*) Two boatloads. He'd have a big, big boat. He'd

take—if we had a pig, he'd take that in the boat—a number of children. And then the other boat—my brother would have the other boat. And the rest would go with him.

(*Was the house at White Point as good a house as you had…?*) No, it was just a summer home, just a summer home. Just two bedrooms, and the kitchen—that was all it was. (*And 16 people lived there.*) We all bunked up. My father and mother slept on a little bed over in that corner of the bedroom. And then four or five of the kids slept on another little bed down this way. Then there was another bed up above them. There were three or four of us, or five of us, slept in that. And then they had another one above that—my brother slept in that. That was just a little bed. We used to go up on a ladder.

(*These beds—were they nailed to the wall?*) Oh, dear, definitely. Oh, yes. Just made like a board—just boards. And a hay tick—used to make the ticks out of those bags. And fill them full of hay. We used to call them the bunk beds.

(*There wasn't a second story to this house, then.*) Oh, no, no, no. It was a flat roof. But it was high. That's all. Just the kitchen. Had a stove, and table. Had a nice large kitchen. **JOHN**: Everybody was comfortable. **SADIE**: Everybody was as happy as could be. **JOHN**: There was no money—no money—nobody had any money.

SADIE: And then you'd all leave, about six o'clock in the evening, and go out squidding. Had to get bait, to go fishing in the morning. They'd go out on what they call "the middle ground." And they'd go out there squidding—they'd stay there till the sun would go down. When the sun went down, then you'd see all the boats coming ashore.

And then, when my father used to codfish, and we'd have to take the fish and carry them on handbarrows up to a flake—had a big flake built. And we'd have to spread those fish out on the flake, and dry them—turn them over three or four times a day—dry them…. In the fall, he had enough fish dried, he'd take them to Sydney and get our winter's supplies. That's how he got his winter supply for the house. He'd take these dried fish to Sydney and sell them. Boatload.

(*He'd jig for squid at night.*) All the men—the middle ground would be black with boats—out squidding for—to get fish in the morning—set their trawls in the morning. (*Would your sisters or you have anything to do with that?*) No. We didn't do anything about that, no. **JOHN**: No, no. Women never worked around fish then. All men. **SADIE**: No. The only thing in fish we worked at is carry them up for the stages, on the handbarrows, and put them on the flake. And we had to tend them. While they were gone, we had to tend them. (*You'd do this right through the fall, I guess.*) Right to till they're dry enough to put away. Maybe they would be on the flake maybe a week—maybe longer if the weather was bad. Because we'd have to cover them with tarpaulins—stack them up and cover them over if it was raining. And maybe they'd be a week and a half on the flake before they'd be ready to pack away....

(*When you say you did it—is that considered heavy work?*) Oh, my dear man. I imagine, it was heavy work. We didn't mind it. We had to do it. Regardless if we minded or not, we had to do it. 'Cause he had no help.

Not us alone—all the women. At that time, all the women helped the men, just the same as the men. They helped mend the nets—we used to mend the nets. Nets'd go out and get torn—herring nets, or salmon nets. Bring them ashore, we'd go down to the stage with them, mend the nets. He'd show us, how to do it. (*But you weren't allowed to do the actual fishing.*) Oh, no, no. No women ever did that.

We'd get up around four, and get all we could done before we'd go to the [lobster] factory. Then we'd work in the factory till five in the evening. (*Now, wait a minute. What did you do from four until you went to the factory?*) Well, the first thing we'd have to do was do the work in the house. We had clothes to wash, we had two tubs and two washboards. We'd have to wash those clothes on tubs and washboard, carry the water from the river, put the wash out, tidy up the house, and help Mother all we could before we'd go to the factory. At seven o'clock we went to the factory. And we didn't get home till 12, for din-ner. Then at dinnertime it was as much as you could do again, before you'd go back again to work. (*You mean work around the house.*) As much as you could get done. As fast as you could go.

Until we'd come back home in the evening. When the factory closed in the evening, we'd have supper. We used to have to carry the water from way up in the mountains—that's drinking water, now. We had to bring the water from the mountain; we had a little well dug up in the mountain. And a little pipe into it. Take the buckets up and fill them full of water. And at that time we used to—the red—I suppose, you often hear talk of red bushes. Like the bushes die, and they turn red. That's what we used to break off—that's when we lived at White Point—we used to go up in the mountain and break armfuls of that and carry it down. That'd be our kindlings for the morning, to make fires out of....

(*And now you've just done a day's work at the factory. Was that heavy work, or hard work, at all?*) Well, it wasn't hard for us. It was tiresome. You stood on your feet all day. We were picking fine meat. (*What does that mean?*) That was picking the meat out of the [lobster] claws, and the arms where you break them there. We had a little, well, the proper little thing. You'd pick all that meat out and put them in a little pan. That was hard work. 'Cause your hands—cracking them, you had your hands all cut. With the knuckles on the lobsters, your hands would be all cut up. (*And was this in cold water you'd be doing this?*) Yes. Cold water. Yeah.

Oh, we always had lots of good stuff to eat. That's one thing he'd always see, that there was lots of stuff in the house to eat. Nobody got hungry. Nobody was ever hungry. Piles of potatoes and fish. And in the fall we'd have a pig to kill, and we'd have a cow or an ox or something to kill—our own beef, and a big pig. And a sheep—we had a whole sheep. We always had piles to eat. That's one thing he'd see.

JOHN: I've been living here since I was seven years old. I'm going on 92 now. And I don't know—I can't remember—a soul on this shore from White Point to South Harbour that ever went hungry. We never had to get relief. Any more than—go to the store and buy the stuff—they might be a little short of money…. But they were never hungry.

SADIE: No, that's one thing would never—nobody was ever hungry. Nobody was ever hungry. My father was a good provider. He looked after everything. When he died, he had money in the bank, after rearing all those children. Yeah, he was a good provider.

(*So White Point would be the go, right through the fishing season, and right into the fall.*) Right to the fall, yeah. (*Now, would you go back as a group, to go home to South Harbour?*) Oh yeah, go back. We'd—there'd be two or three of us walk up with the cattle. We'd take the cows up, the sheep up, from White Point. We'd take them down to White Point and put them down at—we'd call The Hill. We'd put them in pasture down there for the summer. Then in the morning we'd go down there and we'd milk them. Carry the milk home. Then in the evening we'd go back again and milk them. Carry the milk home.

And in the fall, time to come home, take them home—we'd take—three or four of us would take the cattle. Well, only, at that time, maybe there'd be three or four families moving home the same day, eh? Well, we'd all take the cattle in a row, to take them home, see. They'd walk up the road, the cattle and the sheep. We didn't have to put a rope on them at all. Had bells on them. Big bells on the cows' necks.

So maybe there'd be 10 or 11 boats going out of the harbour at one time. Everybody'd move at the same day.

JOHN: They all got together, maybe a week or two weeks before they moved.

SADIE: It was fun, though. It was fun. JOHN: It's not going on now. There's nobody in that line now. All those people in South Harbour are gone now.

SADIE: There were the happy days. Those were happy days, yeah. Because everyone was together at White Point. The little houses were right—you'd step out of one door and step in the other. When they'd move to White Point, the houses were just like that. You'd step from one door to the other. And everybody used to help.

JOHN: You just could get between the houses to paint them—that's all the room there was…. Just room enough to paint between the houses—to paint both sides….

(*Now, I hear stories about getting together in the evenings, singing, making music. I don't see where you'd have the strength.*) SADIE: Oh, we did. Winston Fitzgerald—and Bob Fitzgerald used to play the accordion. And the Newfoundland boats'd come in. They'd be anchored in at the wharf at White Point. And we'd all go down to the wharf, a bunch of us girls. JOHN: Big dance on the end of the pier. SADIE: And we'd have a dance out on the end of the wharf. After we did that we'd all—a bunch of them would walk down to The Hill—White Point Hill—and back again. And walk over to what we'd call The Cove. Walk over there. Well, then it was bedtime. Nine o'clock was bedtime. Then you went home and to bed.

It was beautiful. I'd go all through it again today, if I had to. Every bit of it. We were happy, and we were all together.

To conclude. Let me say a word to the romantic traveller in search of the beauties of nature and yearning for rustic grandeur. When visiting Cape Breton be not content with the tame beauties of the usually travelled routes. Be bold. Starting from Baddeck, journey northward until Cape Smoky has been passed and Ingonish Bay lies in sight. Let the journey be made when the weather is fine, when the sun is bright and summer mists throw their mystic haze over the earth and sea and sky.— from J. W. Longley, "To Cape North," 1892

Dr. LeBlanc's Trek—
Chéticamp to Pleasant Bay, 1936

AT 9 A.M., FEBRUARY 21st, as I was preparing to make a call some four miles south of my home, and debating with myself whether I should take a wagon or a sleigh, a phone call came from Mrs. MacIsaac, the nurse in attendance at the Fraser home, Pleasant Bay Intervale, some thirty-two miles away [heading north].

All I could make out on the phone was that the little patient, a child three years of age, was running a temperature of 103° F, with considerable abdominal distention. Patient had suffered with a severe pain in the region of the 11 rib (left side) the last two days. Called the day before; I had ordered a treatment but with no relief. From the description given by the nurse I feared an abdominal condition so I asked for a few words with the father, which request was granted. I told the father, over the phone, to have the nurse carry on another treatment and to call me by phone at 11 a.m.; I expected then to be at home.

At twelve (noon) I was called; the message had come before my arrival home. The father gave me to understand that the treatment had given no relief to the abdominal distention. I then said, "Call a medical man," and the answer back was, "Will you come?" I pondered for a few minutes and then decided on going, for although my home had been saddened by the tragic death of our dear baby Gerald, an inspiring message seemed to say, "Here is an only child ill thirty miles away seeking medical relief."

I told my family, "I am going to try and help that child, happen what may."

Leaving with my team at 2 p.m. I travelled to Cape Rouge, seven miles north, and stabled my horse at Edward LeBlanc's. Then, with a guide, a lunch and show-shoes, we left Cape

Rouge at 3:30 p.m. I decided to take it easy at first, for not being used to walking, I feared my poor muscles. I walked to the top of French Mountain, a distance of over two miles, a rather icy walk, and rested there waiting for my guide, who was plodding his way up the steep trail with my medical case and lunch.

Before my guide arrived I decided to don the snow-shoes, and try my luck on them. Reaching Jumping Brook I waited for the guide who was trailing his way behind. I asked of him to walk faster. It was then 5:30 p.m. He, unconcerned, replied, "You must not rush yourself." Then I spurted along on my snow-shoes and reached Camp No. 1. Waiting for the guide I said to him, "We must hurry." He replied, "I am taking it easy, so you had better keep ahead and I'll overtake you." Thinking he was sincere I kept on.

At the South Branch of the Fishing Cove

River darkness had overtaken me and in making the turn (or horse-shoe curve) it was impossible to use snow-shoes. Crawling on my hands and knees for about a quarter of a mile, I got to the other side. There I waited for the guide, but after half an hour's wait (I was getting cold), I called out his name a few times but the only reply was my own echo. What was I to do then?

I decided to rush to the Halfway-house and I arrived there at 7 p.m. (It was some three miles from the dangerous curve at the Fishing Cove River.) I sent one of the men from the Halfway-house to meet the guide. A good fire was on so I had a hot lunch. At 7:30 no guide yet. The second man had to go and meet the other two while I remained in the dark. During my anxious hour of waiting I telephoned Mrs. Aka MacLean, Pleasant Bay, and asked her to send men to meet me at MacKenzie Mountain with lights, for my flash-light was about all in.

At 8:15 p.m. leaving George MacLean with my tired guide at the Halfway-house I set out with Herbert MacLean for MacKenzie River. We made good time for in an hour and thirty minutes we were at the Pleasant Bay Lookout. There we were met by Rod Fraser and Dougald Fraser, and good lights. Taking my snow-shoes off I took to running down the Mountain Trail, but I accidentally twisted my left knee in a furrow. Later I accidentally fell on my stomach, which fall did not suit my poor knee.

Reaching MacKenzie River Bridge, Duncan Urquhart was in waiting there for us with his team. I donned two overcoats, covered myself with rugs and the team slid away. After travelling some ten miles I reached Intervale Bridge, a quarter of a mile from the Fraser home. Duncan Urquhart said, "You will have to get off the sleigh." I did, and I was almost a frozen corpse, but I managed to crawl out, and well I did. Then the horse took a plunge, throwing the driver against the railing of the defunct bridge. I was too cold to laugh. Then I decided to crawl on my hands and knees to pass this bridge which had been carried under by the weight of the snow.

Reaching the home I was in order to warm myself and ask for a cup of good Scotch tea.

After warming myself I went to see my little patient. The temperature was 103° F. The distention had gone due to the treatment ordered before my leaving home, and a good bowel movement had resulted. I found after a careful examination that the child was suffering with Pleuro-pneumonia. Gave the treatment and remained at the home until 2 a.m. Then I said, "Men, I am going." We then left to make that long trek. It wasn't very enticing, but I had to get back—a thirty-two mile walk returning.

Larry Fraser, Duncan MacLean and Malcolm MacLean were ready then to accompany me. At 3:30 a.m. we were at the MacKenzie River Bridge. Leaving Malcolm MacLean to take the team back, we set out for the Mountain top. It was then that I felt my left knee to give way, and after a trek of some two miles I could not bend the knee. Determined to make the Halfway-house, I had a hard task to keep up to my two guides though they walked slowly. I was often wishing myself at the wheel of a Ford V8. We got at the Halfway-house at 6:30 a.m. to find my old guide and George MacLean happy and a hot cup of tea ready. My guide said, "I can walk to-day." I smiled and said, "I am crippled up, so call for your dogteam," which he did. After an hour's rest my old guide and I left for the Cape Rouge Trail, while the other men left for their respective homes.

At the No. 1 Camp, I was met by the dogteam and it was time. I could hardly crawl on account of my sore knee. It was then blowing a westerly gale and snowing, which made walking heavy. Then I sat on the dogsled and the dogs trotted along, but coming down the French Mountain it was icy and dangerous, also I suffered discomfort from my knee. I reached the Bourgeois home at 9:45 a.m. It was then snowing heavily and a westerly gale was raging. I rested myself and had a good hot lunch, prepared for me by Mrs. Bourgeois, then I telephoned for my team. Making one call on my way home, I landed at my office at twelve noon. It was then quite rough and stormy.

I rested until 4 p.m. when another call was sent in, but luckily it wasn't far. At 8 p.m. having a nice sleep the telephone again gave me a call, but this time it was only news from my little patient, at Pleasant Bay, reported as resting easy. The next day I was well "all-in."

This is, I think, some of the true hardships of the country practitioner, and to those who have experienced similar treks of sixty-four or more miles in less than nineteen hours, let me repeat the promise of the poet:

> He that ever following her commands
> On with the toil of heart and knees and hands,
> Thro' the long gorge to the far light hath won
> His path upward and prevailed,
> Shall find the toppling crags of duty scaled
> Are close upon the shining tablelands,
> To which our God Himself is moon and sun.

ARCHIE NEIL CHISHOLM TOLD ROSIE AUCOIN GRACE: I was quite young when Dr. Léo LeBlanc was practicing. But I knew much more about him through hearing the stories concerning some of his actions and concerning some of the things he did in the face of terrific odds. And he became almost a legend in his time because if ever a person lived up to the Hippocratic Oath, Dr. Léo did. Because he spared neither himself or his animals, the horses that he drove, nor his cars....

Dr. Léo was born at Margaree Forks.... They were brought up the same as I was—in poverty—they didn't have too much of the world's goods at all. But somehow through sheer hard work and determination, Dr. Léo got through college and got his medical degree. And when he first came to this area he didn't have a house at all. And for some years he stayed at John Alec Chiasson's. They used to call it the Chiasson Hotel. He started practicing from there and, of course, he didn't have a car I don't think. It would be a horse and wagon or a horse and sleigh.

You could see him in the daytime and hear him at night—the old Model T's that—kind of popular—he had one of them. Dr. Léo was a doctor who was highly respected, reputed as being a very good doctor at the time, and he had probably one of the only rivals—I don't mean it in the unfriendly term—one of the only other doctors

in the area at the time was my uncle, Dr. A. W. Chisholm, who lived at Margaree Harbour. There was another doctor, Dr. MacNeil, who was living from about the years 1900 to 1910 at Margaree Harbour, but it was after that that Dr. Léo came in. Safe to say around the '20s, shortly after World War One was over. So he started his practice really living at Margaree Forks, and then he moved to Chéticamp.

But it was nothing to see him driving from Chéticamp to the head of Big Intervale. And that was all narrow dirt roads. The commonest epidemic you had at that time was flat tires from driving over the rocks in the roads. The "rabbit road"—that's exactly what it was. And Dr. Léo went through all of that. I have never yet heard a word from anybody of criticism about Dr. Léo. That is, anything about his personal life. As far as I'm concerned from what my father and mother would say and from hearing other people talking about him, he was a very moral man.

I can remember a particular occasion where there was a young married lady in Northeast Margaree. She was formerly a Gillis from Southwest Margaree and she was married to David Tompkins. They have a very lovely residence in the Margaree area yet. Now, when she was in her third or fourth pregnancy—I know I taught three of her children—it became a desperate situation. There was no hospital in Inverness at the time. It was in midwinter, there were no snowplows on the road, and the result was that the only doctor available to them was Dr. Léo LeBlanc.

Now, it was during a wild stormy day with the snow up over the fences—and I'm not exaggerating that. People as old as I am in Chéticamp will tell you that

that was common to drive on the highway where you couldn't see a fence, the snow would be banked up all winter. Now, somehow they got word through by phone and he started out from Chéticamp.

In the meantime my neighbour, Peter Pat Coady, who would be an uncle to this sick lady's husband—he had a powerful horse and he hitched up his horse and sleigh and started down north to meet Dr. Léo. Dr. Léo got as far as Margaree Harbour when this other man met him. And it was just a matter of jumping out of one sleigh—his horse was played out by that time—into the other.

And I can still see them because we were watching. I can still see Peter Coady and Dr. Léo going out by our place on this terribly cold stormy day and the horse plowing his way just like a sort of a robot through the snowbanks. He spent several hours with this lady—she died, she was still very young—but he didn't lose her through his lack of skill. He lost her as a result of the fact that he was just a little late coming there and the complications had advanced to the point where it was beyond him to save her....

The point that I'm making is that I saw for myself what Dr. Léo would face.

It was another call of mercy that ended his life. He was killed at East Margaree on the road that goes across to the church. Now, I cannot tell you exactly what happened, but from later stories the old Model T—or the cars that they had in those days—had a habit of, if you turned them hard enough, the steering would lock. It was direct steering, it wasn't power steering or anything you have now like that. I believe that's what happened to him. He spun around—and you can see the bank as you're going down from here, the road going over to the church. And it was right coming up that hill where he lost control of the car, or he made the turn too quickly or something like that.

Those are some of the stories. There are others. He was a very charitable doctor. In fact, there's one story told.... You know, doctors got very poorly paid in his day. The doctors were, in some cases, some of the poorest people in the world. And there's one story about him having gone into one house and instead of getting paid he left money with them to get something to eat!

Duncan H. MacDonald's Letter to his Sons

JOHN D. MACDONALD TOLD US the story several years ago. He said that he and his three brothers were serving in Europe during World War Two. And every Sunday night, his father Duncan H. would write a letter to each of his sons. In August 1944, word came to Aspy Bay that Charlie had been killed in action and Gordon was taken prisoner-of-war. The following Sunday, Duncan H. again wrote to each of his sons. This letter was for Charles and Gordon.

August 1944

Dear Charlie & Gordon,

Again on this fine Sunday afternoon we write you these lines as oft we done in answer to your welcome cheerful and never failing letters which Sorry to relate we receive no more and Dear Charlie you have made the Supreme Sacrifice and your body rests far away from your native Shores and Kindred but we trust and Pray that your Soul is at rest with god in his Eternal home and Gordon we Still have hopes that you are Still living and will return to us and if fate Proves otherwise we hope Your soul is in that happy haven.

Tomorrow would be your thirty fifth birthday Charlie and in my minds eye I can Plainly see you as a little lad with your little Pail carring cold water from the old Spring later Plodding to Post Office for our mail and telling us Tall Stories of the Germans you had met on way and destroyed later on but when Seven years old travelling miles to School alone then later in years leaving the Parental roof and going to North River lumber Wood later on to wheat fields of Alberta then home again on the Rawleigh

Duncan H. MacDonald's Letter to His Sons

Route with your faithful horse Jumbo.

Thence to Gypsum Plant at Dingwall and when I heard our country was at war I well knew by your ideals you would be one of the first loyal boys that would enlist for country & freedom and it takes lots of courage to leave home loved ones and friends and embark on the great adventure you and all your brothers we well knew would be in ranks only ye did not wish we be left alone and we are Proud to be the Parents of Such a family but we miss the empty chairs. But ye got your Patriotism honestly from your forebears. Well do I remember being thrilled by father with the tales of the exploits of Nelson at Trafalgar Wellington at Waterloo Wolfe at the Plains of Abraham and in our countries early days Singing the Praises of MacDonald Tupper and Cartier and you Charlie visiting travelling a long way to see the home of your ancestors all goes to Prove that your heart was true and you gave your Precious manly life fighting to the last for us and the freedom you believed in greater love hath no man then that he gives his life for his friends you will always live in our memories as one of natures gentlemen a friend of all and a Son any Parents and Brothers and relatives may well be Proud to own Kinship to and its Sad to See So many of the cream of our country go under but Such is cruel war.

The four MacDonald boys at war. Clockwise from top left: Norman, Gordon, John D., Charlie. Charlie was killed the day after D-Day. Gordon was taken prisoner-of-war.

So farewell Dear Son for the Present but we trust and Pray we will all meet again over yonder where there will be no more Parting and cruel war which Parted us from a loving faithful Son and Brother we'll see no more.

From Father, Mother and Brothers

The Cabot Trail in Black and White

IN MEMORIAM

You left us Sweet Memories Charlie
Deeds of Kindness entwine your Name
We now you are Safe in Heaven
But we miss you and love you the Same
for no hand like yours was So willing
no heart like yours So true
no Son was ever more faithful
or brother more Kind than you
you gave your life to your country
To you all the World owes a debt
But you were ours we'll Remember
Though al the world forgets

        Mother Dad & Brothers

FROM DUNCAN H. MacDONALD'S DIARY:
May 2nd: Set nets. 5th: Two plaster boats. 6th: Shovelled snowbanks. 26th: John D. wounded in Italy. 27th: Put in potatoes. June 3rd: Strong N.E. wind with rain and snow. 6th: Allies start invasion of France. 7th: Charles and Gordon reported missing in action.... July 5th: Christy left for Sydney. 8th: Thomas MacDonald killed in action. 18th: Began haying. August 8th: Received word that Charlie was killed in action June 7th. Sept. 1st: Christy and Robert to Sydney. 2nd: Johnnie Wilkie, Joe Alex and I to Sydney Mines. Sept. 6th: N.D. wounded in Italy. Oct. 6th: Charlie MacAskill wounded in France. Finished digging 32 bushels. John A. MacNeil killed in action, France.

Duncan H. MacDonald and his wife Flora Willena, who was nicknamed "Robert"

Coming ashore at Wreck Cove

Marion Horton
—Bird Islands Life

I WAS A CHRISTIE from Englishtown. I knew of Bird Islands [Ciboux and Hertford] growing up, but I was never there. It wasn't the sort of place people would take a trip to. But I married John Horton from New Campbellton and I went out to Bird Island in 1933. He was already lightkeeper out there. His mother was out there with him. She used to go out and do the baking and washing and what was to be done. He had an assistant lightkeeper at that time—so if John came ashore for a weekend or a few days, he'd attend to the light. (*So when you met John Horton, you knew if you fell in love with him you were going to end up on Bird Islands too?*) Yes, I knew that. And I never regretted it. I never minded living out there. Never.

Well, just like anywhere else, you had your children to look after. Just like anywhere else, you get used to it. Like we would never see anyone from about December until the drift ice would go in the spring. And the drift ice used to stay in an awful long time then. Not like today. Oh my, I remember one time there were 28 days at a time we had drift ice in, jammed up solid. We didn't get any mail. We didn't see anybody. And we had no communication with anybody, no phone. We didn't have a radio until the war broke out, because then they would send messages over the radio—to light up the light or not to light it. But that radio, you wouldn't talk to anyone on it. Just an ordinary radio. No way of communicating with anyone on shore.

I've stayed there alone with the three children for four days one time. And I had to operate the light myself. But I did it. Just in the fall, when the weather would get rough. Once the war started, everybody was gone. See before, any time we wanted to get ashore, we could get an assistant lightkeeper—would go out for a few

days while we went ashore. But the last three years we were there, you couldn't get anybody. So when my husband would go ashore—and if there was a storm come up—well, we were just there till he'd get back. He'd maybe plan to just be in for the day, for supplies—and maybe by the evening there'd be such a sea on he couldn't land on the island. Might be able to get out but wouldn't have been able to land.

Oh my dear, I can remember two or three times that happened. It was the old lighthouse. And you'd have to get up every two hours through the night. You had to wind this weight up to the top—and when it would hit the floor it would stop and your light would stand. Well, you couldn't permit that. And you had to pump air and carry oil up and do all this. Well, the children would be asleep and I would just lock the door, go out and do the job. You had to do it. You always had the lifeline from the lighthouse to the house to hold onto. Oh gosh, yes, you'd have to do that. The wind would be that bad.

(*And the children on days like that?*) Well, they didn't get outside on days like that. Or we had a little harness for them, and we used to tie them to the ring bolt at the lighthouse or the house. Give them some rope. You wouldn't just let them out, unless you could go with them. (*Even when the weather wasn't bad?*) Oh no. The island isn't that wide. And you know a child; if you had something else you had to do, you had to tie them. But they never minded. They never knew any way of running around, I suppose—they were very contented.

Oh, you'd have to have a lot of care. Like through the night, if you were there alone—well, if you had to tend to the light and they cried— they'd just have to cry till you get back. But you'd lock the door and see there was no fire on, just look around there was nothing to harm them. (*Every two hours?*) Every two hours. And you would worry—I wonder if they woke up or what

they did—but still in all, you couldn't let your light stand.

I used to stay out there till about two weeks before the children were born, and I'd go ashore and I'd have my baby. I had a sister at Little Bras d'Or. I never saw a doctor till after I'd have the baby. But I always had a doctor, yes. And when the baby was 10 days old, I went back out to the island with it. But that was one good thing out there—you never got a cold. You never got a cold out on the Bird Islands. (*But if you did need a doctor?*) We used to go across to Point Aconi and go up Bras d'Or Gut and there was a doctor at Little Bras d'Or. (*And when you'd do that, both you and your husband would have to leave?*) Sure we would. And all the children. (*And have to be back that evening?*) Oh, yes. And you know, I stayed out there eight months one time and I never came ashore. I would just as soon stay there as have to take them all in the boat.

(*You had one child sick that you had to bring in in the wintertime.*) Well, she was eight months old. Only an infant. I don't know whether it was from the water or what—but she took something in the stomach, I guess. Diarrhea and throwing up. I knew she was sick. The drift ice was packed in so tight we couldn't get ashore. It was the 4th of April we finally got in. And we left the island

**Hertford Island—
one of the Bird Islands**

at eight o'clock in the morning. (*Took everybody?*) Oh, yes, one other child then. She was about three. We left in a dory. And we rowed around drift ice. And we got into Englishtown at five o'clock in the evening. Eight o'clock in the morning till five in the evening. John was rowing. And his hands were blistered—I'm telling you— and I just held the baby. She was sick for about a week before we got in, but the drift ice was so bad we couldn't get in, and we had no way of getting in touch with anyone—couldn't get a doctor or anything. What is it?—five miles to Bras d'Or? Went in weaving around drift ice.

We got Dr. MacMillan to come down to see her. And he got as far as—well, he was calling right around; he was in South Haven that night—there were just step holes for the horse, just where another horse had stepped. And he didn't get to Englishtown till the next day, there was that much snow. Of course, she was too far gone then, by the time the doctor got there. But Dr. MacMillan came. But it was too late.

It was hard to go back to the island, after that: sure it was. (*But you did go back.*) I went back, yes. And I had two more children after that.

(*That's a lot of courage.*) I don't know. I stayed there year 'round for 11 years, and there's lots of people ask me today how come I ever went there. And I say, well, I guess I didn't know any better. But really, it was a job, I guess. We had a good house to live in. I suppose that was it. Work wasn't that easy to get. The Depression was on and all. Those that had a job were pretty lucky. And if you came ashore, well, what were you going to do? That's what we stayed for—was just the job. I have no regrets about it. As far as saying, well, I'm sorry I ever did it—no. Eleven years, and we never missed lighting the light. I don't think it hurt a person. But you'd be darn glad to get a person and get all the news in the spring.

We liked it there. My husband liked it. But we were very lucky we came ashore when we did. He fished the next spring and the following March—we were only ashore about a year when he had a fatal heart attack. Now if we'd have stayed there, what an awful mess we would have been in in March.

It was just the grace of God itself alone that we came ashore. I often say it was God himself that sent us ashore.

Ulysses LeLièvre, Chéticamp

Pushing Off at Wreck Cove

AT ONE TIME, ALL AROUND CAPE BRETON, fishermen in each community depended on one another to get their boats launched and hauled up again—not only at the beginning of the season, setting the traps, but every fishing day.

The boats, of course, were smaller then, and in many places there was no harbour at all. They'd meet at the shore in the morning, wait to see that one another got off—there'd be a lot of men around; usually two to a boat—and when the last boat got off, all the pushers would jump aboard and get out themselves. And getting in, one fellow would get ashore and man a donkey engine in the winch house—in earlier years it was a capstan—see to it the poles were in place, while the captain watched for the right wave to come in on. A bunch would be gathered there to be sure she didn't go sideways, get swamped and lose her catch. Larger boats and bigger motors, the centralizing fact of the buyer, fewer men fishing in certain areas, and so forth, meant the end of this pushing off together, waiting out weathers, waiting for the last man to come in through the fog. These photographs were taken during the last years there was a crowd pushing off and landing at Wreck Cove Shore. The grounds are still fished but the men use the man-made harbour at Little River. And in the spring there is no activity at Wreck Cove Shore, none at all.

The boats were drawn up over poles laid down before the incoming vessel. Sometimes the winch engine would fail. And even when it didn't, if the shore was bad men would rush forward even before the winch could take up the slack, grab hold of the boat and take her away from the sea.

Below: Dan Murdoch Morrison,
Donald Morrison, D. J. Morrison,
Donnie Morrison, Ian MacDermid,
Stephen MacDermid, John William
Morrison, Hector MacLeod, Roddy
Hector MacDonald, Alexander
Smith—Wreck Cove.

With Lexie O'Hare at Big Intervale

LEXIE WENT TO BOSTON when she was about 18, worked as a nurse, cooked in a logging camp, ran a restaurant and, after her husband died, ran a chicken farm and guest house in New Hampshire. She often returned to Cape Breton, and finally retired to Big Intervale.

We lived there [Forest Glen]. There were six of us at that time. And we could turn out a lot of work—those of us that wanted to work. And some didn't. They didn't like the farm. I left. (*Why?*) Well, my sister [Mary] was getting married and I was going to go and be their bridesmaid. I was a good worker on the farm and that was my pay, that was my vacation after haying and the farm work was all done. (*Had you always wanted to go to the States?*) Well, my sister did. She left three years before that. And writing back and forth—and she was having a good time and buying clothes. They didn't pay too much money at that time but things were lots— and she'd send me things. And I wanted to go.

So I went. (*Alone?*) No, I went with the two girl friends that worked there, that were home visiting their people during their vacation.

(*You were just about 18 years old.*) That's right. I was excited, of course. I thought I knew quite a lot about it from others who had been going back and forth, looking forward to seeing them the next year. I was a young girl. There were a lot of people there who had gone away years before and married and had families. (*Had you thought you were going to stay or just visit?*) That's what my mother thought, too—that I was just going up there for a visit. But I don't know, my sister, she'd like to have me there, because she said, "You'll never get anything on a farm"—and all this business. So anyway, I went. (*Did she mean a man?*) No. Just work. You never could go out and work and earn some money. You'd farm home, but there's nothing for it....

I had my parents [in Cape Breton]. I had been home that summer [probably 1936] and built this little house—had it built—and moved my parents off of the big farm [in Forest Glen]. My mother was 88 and my father was 81. And I had to have something else—what these two hands could do—to support them. So I went to New Hampshire....

(*Where were you born?*) About five miles further north from here—Forest Glen—small farming community. There were about 30 families.

From, say, the red bridge over to the top of the mountain at Grand Étang, Pembroke Lake. We went to school beyond Pembroke Lake. About a mile and a half. All the people in that community went to the same school. But you know, many times, especially after I go to bed—all those families are gone, just passed away. And the younger ones moved away. I don't believe I can count two that I know that their children are living today. They moved to Sydney. Woodbine, Meadows, and whatever they are called. There were about three families of Pembrokes, two families of Campbells, two families of Rosses. There were Camerons, there was Gillis—all gone.

See, they all had small farms, and it was hard to make a living on them. And the children grew up, they just wanted a little bit more, and they didn't stay too long. An awful lot of the young people went to Boston. Because many years before that, there were people did the same thing, and they had relatives there. And I don't remember of anybody at that time going to Toronto. My dad when he was young went to Pennsylvania, and in the wintertime they'd go to the Maine woods, then come home. Try to clear some more land. Mother and the children had the carrying on with the work all winter. And that was about it. All these people I knew were very much in the same thing: small farms, the children leaving very early in life, and old people, taking them away, moving them nearer some city....

My dad in the wintertime went away. He worked 20 years for R. H. White's. That's when they had the farm out Chestnut Hill—horses at that time. I suppose he probably was a stable boy. He worked there all winter. We had a little more cash than neighbours who didn't go away.

My mother was a very, very strong person. She was only a little bit taller than me. But she was as strong as any man you ever saw. And she taught us to do the same thing. And she was very capable. She lived to be 102 and six months. Farming, plowing, cutting wood—the whole responsibility was right there. She could lift a barrel as easy as I could lift a bucket of water—198 pounds. (*Flour got where?*) Grand Étang. There

was a good rough road. They had mills. There were three sawmills right on the Big Intervale. They carried all their boards—lumber—over to Chéticamp, and that was shipped off by boat.

I walked over to Grand Étang when I was 10 years old. That's where all the stores were—the Jersey stores. And we didn't think too much of it. It was great going; we'd call in at all the places. And we were friendly with all the French, because they had no lumber for their boats, sailboats—and we had the lumber. We bartered, you know—they'd give us fish. Everybody was great givers in those times. Nobody went without anything if anybody else had anything. They shared everything. And helped.

(*With your father away so much, your mother must have done a lot of the work.*) Yes. And the children. There was just a cleared piece of land. And he cleared all the rest himself. My father and my mother. The first potatoes we had were planted where the trees were cut. They planted potatoes all around the trees. We had to enlarge the farm. Oh my father, you know— "There's lots of land there," you know, "make another field of hay, and have another cow." Things like that. Saw the tree off. We all learned to use [the crosscut saw]. I was the best one. My father'd rather have me on the other end of the saw than any of them. I wasn't heavy on it.

They'd cut the trees off. And he would bore holes in the stumps, and he'd fill it full of kerosene. Watch it carefully. He'd only do two or three, that he could watch. That would burn out the roots. And made that charcoal. Then the next spring they'd plant potatoes there. Around that. And all the goodness of the soil, and the charcoal from the burning of the wood. And they'd be good potatoes. Then the next year, the roots are all pulled out, and it'd have to be plowed first and then harrowed. Then they planted, I believe, potatoes, and then the next year it'd be oats, and the next year it'd be timothy. And then he'd start another piece of land.

My father made all our shoes, and that's how I learned the trade—I was with my father, and he was my buddy. Mary had Willie, Rachel had John, and Maggie was a baby. He made our lasts out of hardwood. We had to kill the calves, newborn calves. My father would take us to the woods. We had to get bark off the trees, and we had to shave it right small and soak it in water. Soak the calfskin in that, and that would take the hair out of it. Then they tacked it on a building, you know, stretched it, and it made beautiful pink leather. Well, that's the part that went in the shoes—he made shoes for us from that. He could buy copper things to go around the toes here, so you wouldn't scuff them in the stones and that. Of course, as we grew older, well, we'd use the next one's lasts, if our feet were growing. But we went barefooted an awful lot. And my feet are just like my hands. I can do that with all my toes. (*Spread them out like that.*) There isn't a bunion, there isn't a callous, there isn't a corn.

(*Were things ever seen in Forest Glen, unusual things?*) Yes, they used to see a lot of things. I'm psychic, myself. There's things that happened, as a child. When my father used to go away in the wintertime—this was the very first I knew. We had a great big red collie dog. And you know, a dog in those days was one of the family. We thought so much of it. And he always—this night he wouldn't come in. I slept with my mother and Maggie—you know, she was a baby at that time. And the dog started barking. And I said, "My father is coming home tonight."

Now, we didn't know he was coming. We didn't hear. Probably got a chance and didn't know. Usually he would let us know. I said, "He's at the lower field right now." She said, "Oh, sshh—keep still, go to sleep." "He's at the upper field now." And we had a cold spring and a brook. The brook we used for every day and the cold spring we used to be drinking. And I said, "He's at the cold spring right now." After a while I said, "He's at the brook now. And now," I said, "he's at the barn." I said, "He's stepping on the piazza." With that we heard the bang on the door. And I jumped out of bed and there was my father. Now that's the first I've ever. But I didn't think too much of it.

They call it psychic now. (*What did they call it when you were small?*) Ghosts. And people used to hear things.

(*Did you yourself ever see or hear anything that you didn't understand?*) I don't see or hear. It comes into my mind. It can be good—never anything bad. But I didn't understand it.

After my brother Willie died—he lived alone, he was a character, you know. He got into bad company when he was young. He had a habit, you know, of having a little bit too much to drink. He was a likable fellow. He'd come back and say, "Lexie, I'm so glad to be back here, I'm going to kiss you." And he hated kissing—nothing shmush about him. That's the only time anyone got a kiss from Willie, was me. He'd be so glad to get back here. He didn't like it. He lived alone. And he'd get lonesome. He had a couple of old friends, and they liked to drink. He used to love us kids and used to give us money for doing stunts for him. That was all right. I forgot about that.

And here this past winter, just a year ago, I discovered the Shake-and-Bake they had in the stores, you know—for chicken. I suppose you use it and have it. So I'd cook a chicken every week, sometimes twice a week, cook it up, bake it in the oven, put this Shake-and-Bake on it. So I took this terrible itch, went crazy, tearing myself to pieces. Somebody said, "You always have bacon and eggs for breakfast—it's the bacon, cut out the bacon." I cut out the bacon. I cut out the eggs. And I was very fond of cream cheese—I cut out the cream cheese. I cut out everything, and the itch lasted.

So here, about two months ago, I went to bed, fell asleep. I woke up—and I was in the house I was born in in The Glen. And it was just as it was the day Mother and I were the last two to leave....

But I didn't come in the front door. There was a pantry and flour barrels and things, and stairways going upstairs. I came that way. And the front door was like that. And all this side of that was solid people, so happy, laughing. And we had a sink—it was a wooden sink, you know—and there was a bench—we used to keep an extra bucket of water there. And this bench was there. There was one person sitting on that bench. She was dressed quite young, different to the others. And I stood looking at the happy people—and they were so happy and so, just, entertaining to one another. But this one on the bench rose and stood up and walked over to me, and she said, "You know, it's the Shake-and-Bake you're putting on your chicken that's giving you this itch." Everything vanished, just like that.

I cut off the Shake-and-Bake—no more itch.

(*Were you in a dream?*) Not like a normal dream. I sleep and I wake up knowing I was dreaming. It doesn't appear like that. It's like I'm real, I'm just there.

(*And about Willie, he lived with you awhile in Massachusetts?*) Yes. In Boston. 1925-26. (*He had a little drinking problem?*) Yes. And I took him away. My parents were worried about him. He'd go away and he'd take a team, you know— they wouldn't know where he was. But he had friends and he'd always get home. (*So you took him away to Massachusetts, and he lived with you.*) Yes. And my husband got him a job at the Commonwealth Chevrolet. And when he in time appeared the next summer [in Cape Breton], he knew my father couldn't make it—200 acres and two barns. My dad was getting old then. So Willie went home. And he never went back to the States. He died here, four years ago. (*A long time later?*) A long time later is right.

What puzzled me, wasn't it funny, that it

Lexie's parents: Donald M. and Catherine MacLeod Ross

was a Boston street, where Willie lived with me—why wasn't it here? Why wasn't it up at his house?

A short time after he died: I had just got up like I did when I lived there [in Massachusetts]. And the apartment was exactly the same as when I lived there in 1926. Exactly the same. Well, it must have been in my dream. I was just going around and I heard a knock on the front door. [Lexie knocks three times on the table.] I walked over and I opened the door and Willie was there. And he had his hand out and I said, "Oh, Willie." He was in the vestibule. (*And there were other people too?*) Yeah, but they were all to one side, and he was standing at the door and he had his hand out when I opened the door.

And you know, he was dressed just like we laid him away. And he looked wonderful. I gave him the brown suit. And I wasn't a bit surprised. I said, "Willie, let's go sit down." And I caught his hand, and I was just leading him over to the window seat—this is where we used to sit and look out at what was going on down below—and everything disappeared.... (*And the people in the hallway?*) Happy. The happiness on their faces. And I couldn't hear a word they were saying, but they were just so busy talking—but the expression on their faces!

And the same thing happened here a couple

of months ago with the Shake-and-Bake. And you know, I went to bed and I'm thinking, That must be Mary—you know, my sister—she was only 22 when she died. But before she died, she didn't look [like the girl I saw]. I have a picture of her with her husband. She was a great, great girl. I always wanted to be like she was, but that never was to be. She was the most wonderful person, wherever she went, she was dearly, dearly loved. There wasn't a boy in the country anywhere but had a crush on her. And you know, she was jolly and witty and she never really cared.

[The next day, visiting with Lexie again, she said she was glad we had talked about the Shake-and-Bake story. When she went to bed afterwards, she realized it wasn't her sister Mary who had given the information, it was a little girl she knew in the States.] They had this little girl. They were a very very very nice couple—the father and mother—it was marriage formed for them. She never met him until she met him in the States—you know, they pick their wives for them—the gentleman's father and mother. And he married a very lovely Jewish girl. And I got acquainted with them. We were wonderful friends. And they had a little girl and she was born with club feet. Dear little thing, they used to bring her into the store to see me. And I fell in love with her and she fell in love with me. She'd be wanting to come in to see Lexie and they'd take her in. So they had different operations on her feet—feet kept turning back. She was a smart, dear child. There was a place in Colorado where they were promised a cure. But they needed the money and they didn't have the money. But I loaned them the money to send the child there. And the operation was successful and the feet stayed straight. One morning they went up—she didn't get up at her usual time—and they found her dead in bed. It was too much strain on the heart, all those operations. You know, I never forgot that child. I still see her plain as when she used to come in the store.

(*As a young girl, how did you learn about sex?*) I never heard the word until—I never heard the word sex in the States. We were very very very modest. I wouldn't undress in front of my sister. We had to blow the lamp out. I was a tease, I was devilish, you know. And my brother'd be fishing—Willie—and he'd get soaking wet. 'Cause they used to wade the pools, you know. (*He'd be fishing for salmon?*) Oh, [and] trout—you could fish all you wanted to, you know—and even the brooks were full of trout. I used to go along with him when he fished the brook, to carry the trout. (*There was that much of it?*) That much of it—two gads—we used alder gads. It's a bush with two branches on it. You cut it down and trim it, and you slip the head of the trout on that. I'm so short that the trout would be dragging on the rocks. We'd only have to go about a mile to get those. The river was so full of salmon, in my mother's day, the horses used to slip on them and fall down. They'd cross the river on horseback—there was no bridge. And she'd—you know the bread pan—you know, they made bread every day—she'd take that when they wanted a trout or a salmon, and go down to the river, scoop one up. Anywhere, anytime. The river was teeming with trout and salmon. And they lived right near the river. The brook here, and the house here, and the river there. And then they had a great big freshet separated the barn from the house; then they had to build another barn. That's where the river is today.

(*You were telling me how modest you were….*) I was a tease. My brother would come home soaking wet and he'd go upstairs to his room. And he'd holler down, "Throw up my dry pants." And I'd go to the foot of the stairs, pretending I was climbing. He said [shouting], "I thought I told you throw them up! Throw them up!" I said, "They won't go over the bannister—I'll walk with them." [Lexie making a thumping sound like going up stairs.] "I'll throw you out the window," he says, "if you ever come up here!"

(*No one ever told you about sex?*) Nobody ever ever ever did. (*When you were going away to the States, didn't your mother take you aside?*) No. She went out the night before and she wanted to cry. I looked out and I saw her way down in the field and I ran and I caught up with her. You know, she had an apron on, she wiped the tears—she didn't want anyone to see her cry. I asked her what the trouble was, Mother. "Nothing, just I'm going to miss you so much. I'm not going to worry about you, Lexie, because you were always a good girl"—and that was all she ever said to me.

(*How long were you actually married?*) Eleven years. We went together 10 years. And we never had a quarrel. (*Aw, that's not true.*) That's the truth to God. We never quarreled. There was nothing to quarrel about. But I think he had plenty. I could go to the dances with the girls, I could do anything I wanted to, I could come home here and stay the summer if I wanted to.

(*You didn't marry again after your husband died.*) I had my parents—they weren't making any money on the farm. I had to help them too, you know. (*You were sending money home?*) Oh, always, always. All my life from the first dollar I ever made. And I had Raymond. I never loafed a day through the Depression, but I didn't make much money, you know, but it was something.

(*Why did you come home to stay?*) My mother was 88 years old, and she had my dad here alone, and he'd had a heart attack before. That's what made me move here in 1943. I was home in June 1936, and they moved in here in September. And I came home in '43. They were here by themselves. But my sister was near. And my mother was smart. She did all her own baking up until that time, and got the meals. She even took her brother in as a boarder, her last winter here.

(*You sold everything in New Hampshire?*) Not at first. I rented it. I thought perhaps to live here a year or two years. I didn't think that Mother would live 16 years after that. I was going to go back. I rented it. So in two years time Mother was stronger than ever. I was here doing all the work. So I just went back and I sold it.

I came back to Cape Breton, and we lived on. And lived on and on and on, for 16 years. Father passed away in '45, but Mother lived till '58.

William Roach,
folk artist,
Petit Étang

Clarence and the Whales

CLARENCE BARRETT, *Middle River*: One calm summer evening I was drifting along the western shore of the Park in my canoe, making my way back from Fishing Cove. High red sandstone cliffs towered above me, turning redder as the sun got lower. The sea was like mercury, reflecting the blue and gold and crimson of the sky and sunset. The only sounds were the splash of my paddle and the wheezy *peeeeee* of a black guillemot swimming on the surface ahead of me. As I glided toward it, the little puffin-like seabird ducked its head into the water, making sure it was safe to dive, and with a quick beat of its wings disappeared under the surface. There was a momentary glimpse of its white wing patches as it used its wings to "fly" through the water. It bobbed back up a little distance away but I was still heading for it. This time when I got too close it ran along the surface of the water until it could lift off, and with its bright red legs trailing behind, it circled around me a couple of times and landed again, satisfied that I was no threat.

Paddling close to the cliffs I could see down through the water to where rock crabs and sea stars rested on the bottom. As I drifted around a sea stack a startled great blue heron lifted off a barnacle-covered rock and flapped away in slow motion toward Chéticamp Island. I paddled back out from the shore, into the empty, glimmering expanse toward the horizon where I could get a better view of the hills behind the cliffs. I've heard the term "aquellae" suggested to describe those myriad flashes of light created by the reflections of sunlight on the dimpled surface of the water, and that the sea was "brinkling" when it did this. The scene was so magical I wanted to stay out on the water as long as I could.

The smell of wood smoke from the campfires at the Corney Brook campground drifted over the water, and I saw people gathering on the bank above the shore to watch the sunset. Some of them were pointing seaward. At what? People were beckoning to others, and as more people gathered to look I stood up in the canoe to try to see what they were looking at. The trail of light on the water leading towards the sun made it difficult.

Then I saw them—pilot whales! The black arcs of their backs broke the surface about 300 metres away. Again and again they broached, sometimes singly, sometimes two or more at a time. There must have been dozens of them. Suddenly, directly in front of me, not six metres away, the bulbous forehead of a whale shot up at a low angle out of the water and then plowed back in, followed by the long gentle arc of the glistening body. I sat down in the canoe, grasping the gunwales, wondering what to do. I had paddled pretty far from shore, intending to drift back in with the slight sea breeze. Behind me there came a hissing sound, as of a slight turmoil in the water, and I turned in time to see the black, rubbery dorsal surface and the fin slip beneath the waves.

They were all around me. And they seemed to be having so much fun, as if they were taking part in a sort of marine loppet. There was a mother and her calf, the two of them broaching and diving in unison. The whales seemed benign and playful with their permanent carefree smiles, and they showed no particular interest in the canoe—but what if one of them was to accidentally surface under the canoe? In any case, if I was going to be upset it was too late to do anything about it at that point, so I just sat and watched the show. In the end, they passed by with what seemed almost deliberate courtesy by not crowding the canoe, and once again it was just me and the guillemot floating in the twilight.

With Bay St. Lawrence behind him, Ryan Yoshi on the road to Meat Cove

"Like I was saying, the Cabot Trail created not only wonders for each family but for the area as a whole. It also made a big change for the people here themselves—they got to know each other more."— Joe Delaney to Judith V. Campbell, 1973

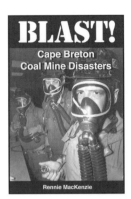

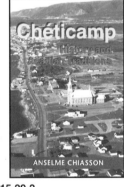

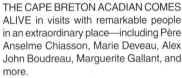